Why Didn't Somebody Tell Me This Stuff?

Stuff?

100 tips on how to work, fight and schmooze your way to the top!

A new employee's guide to adapting to, competing in and excelling in corporate America

By Christopher J. Andrews

Table of Contents

Introduction

As a manager of many young professionals throughout my career, I have sort of developed a personal pattern of taking all of my new hires out to lunch on their first day. I use these luncheons to formally welcome the new employee to the group and to initiate an on-going dialogue about what the organization expects of them, and what I expect of them as a professional. While cordial and friendly, these luncheons are no doubt a professional business event and should be treated as such. Nonetheless, others apparently feel differently. I can recall this one young man who was hired just out of college with no prior professional experience. As we sat down at the restaurant and started our conversation, one of his first questions was "So, are there any attractive girls that work in the office." Then, whether he was nervous and trying to lighten the moment with some humor or whether he was simply ignorant in the ways of corporate etiquette, he then proceeded to tell me about some of his most memorable stories from college, many of which involved him in varying degrees of intoxication. While this may be an extreme example, this is nonetheless a true story, and does represent a significant failing of many of today's young professionals. While many recent college graduates may have achieved great accomplishments in the classroom and on their campus settings, the fact is that many of these recent college graduates are totally unaware how to conduct themselves in a professional office and corporate setting.

I am always amused that no matter how often I hold a staff meeting someone, typically a young and recent hire with little professional experience, will show up at the meeting with absolutely nothing in their hands; no pad, no pen, no date book or PDA, etc. I'm not quite certain what they think we are going to be discussing, but meetings are generally called to disseminate relatively worthwhile information. In many cases this information is time sensitive in nature and it routinely involves some form of detailed instructions to those members in the meeting. In such cases, I will purposely make the instructions complicated and intricate so that they are forced to scramble for a piece of paper to write them down in haste. Some people just do not understand proper professional etiquette and what the corporate world expects of them. In all honestly, it is not entirely their fault, because there are very few resources available today that actually teach young men and women who are entering the corporate world, the inside story on how to properly conduct themselves so they can assimilate and excel in their roles as young professionals. Many central practices and rudimentary expectations, which are widely accepted in the corporate world as "simply understood" and a "given" by seasoned professionals are rarely taught by parents, professors, career counselors, colleagues, co-workers, or even the employee's immediate supervisor or manager. That is where this book comes in. This book does not discuss tips and strategies on *obtaining* a job (e.g., interviewing tips), this book discusses tips on how to succeed once you have obtained a job. This book discusses critical strategies for integrating into corporate culture, successfully promoting yourself, developing a favorable reputation, building strong political capital and so forth, each of which will assist you in quickly climbing the corporate ladder of success.

Over the course of my career I have worked with many young employees who have been hired straight out of college or business school. I have also worked with many young employees who had very limited experience in the corporate world (e.g., less than five years). I often refer to these individuals as "young professionals." Young professionals may have outstanding grade point averages. Young professionals may have degrees from very impressive colleges or universities. Young professionals may have extraordinary resumes and may have very polished interviewing skills. Young professionals may have achieved significant technical knowledge throughout the course of their educational career. They may fully understand the intricacies of discounted cash flow analysis, financial and managerial accounting, statistical sampling methodologies and so on. However, the fact of the matter is that young professionals are all too often inexperienced, untrained and unproven with regard to the inner workings of the corporate world. What is worse is, unlike their educational careers, there really is no one responsible for instructing them on these matters. As they begin their journey through the challenging landscape of today's corporate world, they are all too often on their own. This book is the young professional's compass, helping to guide and direct them on their journey through the treacherous and unforgiving environment of corporate America.

Young professionals must learn how to navigate and maneuver through the labyrinth of office etiquette and corporate politics by themselves. Young professionals must become closely familiar with the demands and expectations associated with working in the fast paced, highly competitive, performance driven environment of corporate America. Clearly, one's experience and a proven track record of accomplishments can only be developed over time; however, young professionals must be sure to properly educate themselves about their new environment and they must commit themselves to developing the necessary tools to excel in this environment. This book identifies many key tips and suggestions that a young professional can easily utilize to help identify and satisfy the often unspoken expectations and needs of their managers, senior executives, employers, and the corporate community as a whole. Being able to successfully isolate and meet these needs will help place the young professional at a tremendous advantage, which will thus allow them to stand out from the crowd and ultimately destroy their competition.

The suggestions provided in this book are far reaching and have widespread applications, which are not specific to any particular form of job, size of employer or type of industry. Regardless of whether you are starting, or have recently started, a career as a banker, attorney, accountant, architect, sales representative, or any other professional position, this book will prove helpful and invaluable throughout your career. This book provides its readers with indispensable advice on how to tackle challenges, develop essential skills, build political capital, create positive standing, develop meaningful contacts, and a whole lot more. In short, this book is intended to act as a genuine survival guide to those young professionals who have decided to venture out into this deep, darkened and dangerous forest that we call corporate America.

Have a Plan

As you embark upon your career, there is little advice that is more important than having an appropriate plan. Failure to do so will leave much of your career development to pure happenstance. One cannot successfully chart and navigate a proper course of action unless they know where it is that they wish to go. Young professionals should prepare for themselves one-year, three-year and five-year career plans. These plans should be in writing and readily available for review. These career plans will act as a career road map, guiding you to where it is you wish to be. These plans will outline the proper routes or courses of action that you intend to utilize in order to arrive at your final destination. When developing your career plans, be guided by the following tips:

- Find your destination. Establish exactly where it is you wish to be in one, three and five years. The more specific you can be the easier it will be to develop appropriate strategies and action plans.

- Establish specific and measurable checkpoint objectives. These are goals that you will likely need to achieve on your way to achieving your final destination objective. For instance, if you are starting out as a junior associate at a marketing firm, and ultimately wish to be a senior project leader within five years, map out all applicable positions and titles that one would typically hold before being promoted to senior project leader. After junior associate, you might consider establishing a promotion to senior associate as one of your checkpoint objectives. After a senior associate, you might establish a promotion to junior project leader as another checkpoint objective. From here, you might consider yourself to be in a position to be considered for a promotion to senior project leader.

- Set specific action plans for each checkpoint objective. For instance, lets say you are a junior associate and have identified a promotion to senior associate as a one-year checkpoint objective. Try to identify those accomplishments that must be achieved or skills that must be developed in order for you to be promoted to senior associate. It may be that you feel that you may need to conceive, market and implement one of your ideas within a major project assignment. It may be that you feel that you may need to improve upon your presentation skills. Whatever the case, be specific about what you need to do in order to put yourself in a position to achieve your next objective.

- Be sure that your destination objective and checkpoint objectives are reasonable and achievable. Destination and checkpoint objectives that are unreasonable and unlikely to be achieved within your budgeted career plan timeline will often diminish one's desire and reduce one's motivation. On the contrary, by establishing reasonable and achievable objectives, one can often help to fuel the fire of one's enthusiasm and motivation. As objectives are established and achieved, one will often gain a much greater sense of confidence and increased motivation to further advance to the next objective.

- Assign a deadline or due date for each major goal or checkpoint objective. In between each objective, establish monthly, quarterly and annual checkpoints to ensure that you are on track to achieve each of your objectives. Doing so will enable you to measure your progress. If you later determine that you are falling behind in your anticipated development schedule, you might consider adjusting your strategies or pursuing other actions such as soliciting additional guidance from your manager or a trusted colleague.

- Review your plan on a regular basis. You should regularly review your plan to remind yourself of where you are headed, and how you are planning to get there. You also need to review your plan to ensure that you are progressing as expected. Try creating a career timeline of your one, three and five year plans with each of your objectives mapped out. Cut out a small picture of yourself and place it at the applicable point on the timeline. Paste your timeline somewhere private but readily accessible and visible to you so that you can physically see where you are according to your career plan. A great idea is to paste your timeline(s) on the inside of your closet door at home. That way, each morning as you open your closet to get dressed for work, you will constantly be reminded of where you are and where you are headed.

- Consider sharing your career plan with your boss. Unless you plan to hold your boss's job as one of your objectives, sharing your plan with your boss will serve you in several ways. Doing so will likely show him or her that you are exceptionally well organized. Doing so will also exhibit an impressive sense of initiative and motivation. Doing so will also enable you to solicit their opinion and thoughts about the feasibility of your plan. Here you can ask them if they feel your plan is fair and reasonable. If not, you have an opportunity to ask them why, and possibly adjust your plan as needed.

Know Your Employer

Having specific knowledge about the history, size, value, performance, *etc.* of your employer can be very useful to a young professional. Understand your company's mission, its market and its competition. Know who the key players are in all major functional areas of the organization. Having a broad understanding of the overall corporate history of your employer will validate your commitment to the company.

If your employer is publicly held, much of this information will be readily available through Securities and Exchange Commission filings, regulatory disclosures, annual reports, marketing material, *etc.,* all of which is made available to the public. If your employer is privately held, you may have more of a difficult time finding information, but there should still be a wealth of data available through the company's web site, marketing material, archived news releases, *etc.*. Speak with employees who have been with the company for a long time. Ask them questions about the company, its culture, its practices and its people. Ask them how things have changed, whether for the good or bad, since they began working with the company. Try doing a simple Google search on your company and its key people and see what type of information you can find.

Having a firm grasp on your employer's history, its mission, its operations and its key employees will exhibit a level of enthusiasm and passion that is not typically seen in younger talent; thus, presenting an opportunity for you to distance yourself from your co-workers. Picture this scenario, your boss, and to a lesser extent you, are involved in an intense conversation with the regional executive about your division's profitability. During the conversation, it is becoming clear to you that your boss is having a difficult time justifying a slight decline in your department's profitability. How do you think that regional executive might portray you when you politely interject and say…?

> "Pardon me Mr. [Regional Executive], I can clearly understand your concerns about our profitability; however, I think it's important that we view our profitability in the context of our overall market share. According to our latest 10Q SEC filing, our market share increased by more than 3.5%, which was the largest quarterly increase in the past 5 years. Additionally, I think it's worthy to note that our latest customer service survey indicates that client satisfaction within our group is the highest it has been in our company's 75-year history. Therefore, if we can

further strengthen our brand, reinforce client loyalty and increase our market share, we might be more successful at enhancing our overall profitability through greater economies of scale, as well as more effective cross-selling initiatives with other areas of the organization."

It's likely that the regional executive will be thinking to himself "Wow! Who the hell is this person?" and chances are that your boss will be thinking "Wow! Why didn't I think of that?"

Equally important to understanding your company's overall mission and history is, understanding the underlying operations, policies, procedures, practices and all other specific intricacies of your particular area or department. How do certain operations work, who is responsible for what tasks or responsibilities? Having a keen understanding of the department, group or division that you work in is essential in identifying inefficiencies or redundancies, and developing appropriate solutions. Doing so will ultimately help you create value, build political capital and develop a strong and favorable reputation for yourself.

Understand How Political Capital Works

Young professionals must understand the intricacies of developing, maintaining and strengthening appropriate and meaningful political capital within the organization. They must also master the art of using the political capital of others to their own advantage.

In short, political capital is the ability to develop a sense of trust, credibility, respect and confidence among those select individuals within the organization who hold the power to influence the organization and ultimately one's career. Political capital acts much like economic capital. Political capital can be earned, or it can be inherited (e.g., CEO's children working at the same company will naturally inherit some degree of political capital within that organization). Political capital can be gained and it can be lost. The more political capital you have the easier it is to assemble necessary resources to meet objectives and overcome obstacles. The more political capital you have the easier it is to weather adversity and hardship.

There are many ways to develop one's political capital; however, the most common ways are to develop a strong and consistent record of performance, exhibiting a strong work ethic, committing yourself to your professional growth and development, demonstrating strong morals and ethics and successfully aligning yourself with key decision makers in the organization.

Understand that political capital may not necessarily be representative of one's title, position, professional experiences or educational background. You may not have an Ivy League education, and may not have been groomed in the organization's most elite training program, but if you can successfully develop a strong and favorable reputation amongst those individuals with meaningful authority within the organization, you will develop a strong base of political capital. Once you have developed a strong base of political capital, you will ensure that your name is mentioned along with those with higher educations and greater experiences when project teams are being assembled or when promotional opportunities are being reviewed. This will allow you to increase your exposure within the organization and greatly enhance your ability to advance through the organization.

As you are developing your own political capital it is equally important that you make efforts to utilize the political capital of others. In many cases, the magnitude of one's political capital is more important than their title or position itself. For instance, imagine two scenarios. The first is a situation where you are working for a senior vice president. However, it is clear to you that this senior vice president has a poor performance record, has a poor work ethic, has a poor reputation throughout the company and has weak relations with the key decision makers in the organization. While this senior vice president may have a high level position within the company, they do not appear to have much political capital. Contrast this with the second scenario. In the second scenario, imagine that you are working for a vice president. However, this vice president has a proven track record of high performance, has a strong work ethic, has lead several successful project teams, holds leadership positions in various trade related organizations outside of the organization and enjoys strong and favorable relations with key decision makers in the organization. Which one of these individuals would you like to work for, champion your cause and prepare a recommendation for your promotion? While one's title cannot be completely disregarded, the level of one's political capital cannot be overlooked either. Young professionals must be sure to develop, maintain and strengthen their own political capital, as well as make all reasonable attempts to align themselves with those individuals who posses strong political capital.

Develop Your "Brand"

The term "brand" represents an identity, a trademark, or a distinction of one product or service from all others. Companies that successfully create a strong and favorable brand for themselves and their products are really strengthening their competitive advantage and are distancing themselves from their competition. The term "brand" applies not just to companies and products, but also to individuals. Young professionals must focus their efforts in the office on developing their own individual "brand."

Developing a strong and favorable brand for yourself is critical to your success. How are you perceived by your co-workers?, your manager?, middle management?, senior and executive management?, your clients?, etc. Are you known as the "hardest working person in the office"? Are you known as "the smartest person in the office"? Are you particularly known for some specific technical skills or abilities, or are you known for having excellent interpersonal skills and strong social attributes? On the contrary, are you known as the "office slacker"? Are you known as a "follower rather than a leader"? Are you known as "one for taking shortcuts and the easy way out of a problem"? Are you known as a proverbial "nine to five'er"? You have complete control over how you are to be perceived within your organization. However, once you have already developed your brand, whether intentionally or unintentionally, whether favorable or unfavorable, it can be very difficult to change this. Thus, it is important that you understand the importance of this at the onset of your career and strive hard to develop the right reputation. How you conduct yourself and how you perform in the office will ultimately help to shape your own individual "brand." Be sure that your brand is one that is positive, productive and a reflection of values, beliefs and principles that are important to your organization. Be aware that to develop a positive and productive brand, you have to earn it, and it does not come easy. A favorable brand is typically built upon a firm commitment to your responsibilities, a dedication to the organization, a strong work ethic and a proven record of consistent accomplishments. While building a strong and favorable brand may be difficult, it is nonetheless an essential weapon that can be used to defeat those competing against you. Successfully developing the right brand can represent a prime advantage when you are competing against others who may have greater political capital, a better education or more experience than you.

Be Prepared To Pay Some Dues

While you may have graduated at the top of your class from a prestigious college or university, this does not make you immune to having to pay your proverbial "dues" as you work your way up the corporate ladder. Corporate America is continuously downsizing and seeking greater efficiencies. With so many recent advances in technology, staff head counts are down, yet demands for increased productivity have never been greater. The days of dedicated personal assistants and excessive administrative help are all but a thing of the past. Many high-ranking managers and executives now must share such support staff. In doing so, they expect their employees to be fully capable and willing to perform certain basic office functions themselves. This may include making a set of photocopies, scanning documents, answering your own telephone, filing documents, keeping your own schedule, typing your own correspondences and so forth. Employees, particularly newer entry-level employees are expected to perform many of these functions by themselves, without the assistance of others. While it is hard to get excited about such duties, bear in mind that you must develop a reputation as team player. Even if you agree to perform such duties, rolling your eyes or offering a deep passive aggressive sigh when asked to do such tasks will send a blatant message that you feel that you are above such a task, so be cautious about how willing you appear when you accept such tasks. You want to be viewed as a person who is willing to roll up his or her sleeves to help the group out. So act accordingly.

There will eventually come a time where you will have reached a certain position within the organization where performing such duties yourself may not be practical or economically feasible; however, until you reach that point, it is important that you willingly and agreeably accept such duties. Pitching in and accepting your role within the group, regardless of how insignificant or monotonous the tasks, will send a positive message that you are capable of seeing the value of your contributions from a broader selfless organizational perspective, rather than from a personal and selfish perspective. If you cannot willingly accept such tasks, you run the risk that others will form an adverse impression of you, which may spread (whether wrongly or rightly) throughout the group and the organization. This will impede your ability to (1) develop an expansive network of contacts, (2) build strong political capital and (3) shape a favorable image of yourself throughout the group and organization.

Ask For More Work

One of my earliest managers once told me that my entire job description could be summed up as simply as this:

> "To help make my life easier and that's it!"

In a sense, this is not too far from the truth. Employees that work hard and produce results, make the lives of those that they report to, much easier.

When time permits and you have a moment or two of free time at the office, rather than sit at your desk looking busy and daydreaming about the weekend, simply approach your manager and ask if you can help him or her with anything else. Indicate that you are caught up on all of your tasks and assignments, and politely inquire if you could assist them with anything in the meantime. Occasionally approaching your manager and asking for additional work sends several positive messages. It shows your manager that you are capable of completing all of your assigned tasks and responsibilities. It also shows your manager that you are a self-starter who truly wants to prove themself as a competent and valued member of the group, rather than someone whose sole purpose is to do as little as possible and whose only real interest is collecting their paycheck every two weeks. It may also show them that you are seeking greater challenges and additional responsibilities, potentially signaling to them that you have outgrown your current position and are therefore seeking, and in need of, advancement.

A word of caution here however, is to be sure that your level of productivity and the quality of your work meets your manager's expectations first before asking for any additional work. If not, focus all of your efforts on developing the skills and talents necessary to perform your primary duties before asking for any additional work. Only once you have mastered your day-to-day primary responsibilities should you start inquiring about additional work.

<u>Don't Compete Against Yourself</u>

Throughout your career you are going to face tremendous competition. You are going to face industry competition from other organizations seeking to steal your clients and market share. You are also going to face inner company competition from those within your organization who may be seeking the same training, development or promotional opportunities as you. However, an equally important, and potentially disastrous, form of competition is what I refer to as one's self-competition. Self-competition essentially represents any and all thoughts or beliefs within oneself that may dilute one's enthusiasm, dampen their spirit, damage their self-confidence or destroy their self-discipline. In essence, self-competition is a failure to believe in one's own abilities and a failure to commit to the necessary sacrifices to achieve a specific objective.

Self-competition is a much larger issue than can be sufficiently covered in this book. Not having a degree in psychology I am also somewhat hesitant to render too much guidance here; however, suffice to say that today's young professionals must truly and completely have the confidence to conquer any obstacle in their way. Failure to do so can be catastrophic in developing one's career. However, having true confidence in one's abilities should not be misinterpreted as arrogance. Having confidence in one's abilities means that one truly and sincerely believes that he or she is capable of extraordinary accomplishments, but also humble enough to recognize that extraordinary accomplishments will often require extraordinary work and efforts. Here is where one's self-discipline becomes essential. Having the confidence is the first step in combating your inner competition. The second step in combating self-competition is having the self-discipline to take the steps necessary to properly position yourself for success. This may mean obtaining certain educational credentials, developing specific talents or abilities or learning a specific skill. Self-discipline is often synonymous with sacrifice. Therefore, young professionals must be willing to make certain sacrifices so that they may better position themselves for success. This could be as insignificant as foregoing the Friday happy hour once in a while so that one can complete their research for a certain project, or as significant as a decision to delay their marriage, or the starting of a family, so that they can complete their graduate levels studies or a specific certification program. That is self-discipline, and it is an essential ingredient to one's success.

Speak Up

Speaking up at an opportune time on a key issue can often have a dramatic impact on one's career. By "Speaking Up" I mean two things.

First, if you have an idea or suggestion, you need to gather the courage to be heard. Many young professionals are hesitant to speak up because they feel that they don't have sufficient experience or knowledge to contribute a meaningful comment to a conversation or dialogue. In some cases this is incorrect and quite the contrary. Due precisely to this lack of experience, young professionals often approach problems with distinctly different perspectives. This is generally because their thought processes have not been completely sanitized by 10, 15 or 20 years of working for the same company, in the same culture, honoring the same policies, the same procedures or the same practices. The minds of these new employees are often fertile with fresh ideas and new perspectives.

Second, by speaking up I am also referring to the volume and confidence in your verbal delivery. Have you ever heard someone make a statement that might be factual and entirely accurate, but the message is delivered in a manner that is subtle, unconvincing and meek? Regardless of whether the message is true, the manner in which it is delivered is unconvincing and can often lead the audience to question the validity of the suggestion, solution or message. When speaking up, be sure to speak with confidence and assurance.

I must emphasize the importance of proper etiquette and professional respect, when speaking up. In other words, you should not necessarily interrupt someone, particularly a senior member of the organization. Wait for an appropriate lull in the conversation, then jump in with your thoughts. You also want to be sure that you are somewhat selective when deciding what matters you wish to interject your ideas and suggestions into, particularly when the matter does not pertain directly to your day-to-day responsibilities. In other words, as a young professional if you interject yourself into an executive level conversation concerning the strategic direction of the organization you might be overextending yourself. Carefully select the issues that are most important to you, and your career, and purposefully insert your ideas and suggestions into those situations. You must also be sure that your ideas are thoroughly thought out and scrutinized for validity and reliability before submitting them. If you make a habit of making suggestions that have already been suggested by others, or recommending solutions that are not technically, operationally or economically feasible, you may be doing yourself more harm than good, as others may view you as someone who does not do their "homework" or perform the necessary due diligence before making a suggestion.

Many people often have the same idea, but are afraid of sharing the idea for fear of being ridiculed or mocked. Many people are also afraid of speaking in a group or public setting. Both of these obstacles are common hindrances that must be removed if an employee wishes to be viewed seriously as a true professional. In fact, in my experience I have often found that when a group of managers are discussing a problem, one person might recommend a solution, but many of the others subsequently admit that they had the very same idea. In other words, the others never had the courage to speak up. In such situations being the first to say what is on your mind may likely improve your chances of being recognized as a leading problem solver. Just do not forget the following rules when speaking up:

- Get the facts. Be as sure as you possibly can that your idea will be effective and is fully feasible.

- Be selective on when you choose to interject your thoughts and ideas. Save your thought and suggestions for the most material issues, which apply most closely with your day-to-day responsibilities. This is not to say that you cannot offer a thought or a comment on other broader topics, just be sure that your thoughts and comments are well thought out and feasible.

- Be courteous and professional when stating your thoughts. Don't interrupt, and if you must disagree with someone, do it diplomatically. Preface your disagreement with a respectful and cordial opening such as:

    o "I understand what Mr. Smith is saying, and sincerely respect his opinion; however, I'm seeing the problem a little differently. For instance, let me explain..."

This delicate and respectful method of disagreeing with someone usually goes a long way toward saving face with that individual.

- Speak with confidence and assurance. This is a direct reflection of the preparations and due diligence that you put into your idea. If you are satisfied that the issue has been thoroughly researched and well thought out, you are much more likely to speak in a persuasive and convincing manner.

- Speak up to be heard. A good rule of thumb is to visualize your audience twice as far away from you as they actually are, and speak to them in a volume that would then be required.

As mentioned earlier, if you follow these rules and are the first member of the group to recommend an idea or propose a solution, you will effectively "own" that idea or solution. That idea or solution will have become yours, and not anyone else's who may have been "thinking the same thing." You will be the one who will be recognized and rewarded for your contributions. So be sure to speak up!

Manage Your Time Well

Time is a precious and finite resource. There is only so much time in each day to accomplish the things that need to get done. Properly managing your time, both personally and professional is essential to a happy life and critical to advancing your career.

It is important that you properly balance your personal and professional time. One should not have to suffer because of the other; however, you might need to be creative in terms of finding room for each. For instance, if you enjoy running you might need to get up extra early to squeeze in that morning run so that you can stay late at work some evenings to finish up a certain project or assignment. If you enjoy playing golf, try using this interest to your professional advantage by inviting some of your coworkers, colleagues or clients to play one afternoon or on the weekend. While playing, you might be able to handle some business while also having some fun. If you enjoy skiing, hiking, kayaking, etc. take out a calendar and mark out a few weekends to dedicate to those hobbies, but pledge to yourself that an equal number of weekends or evenings will be dedicated toward enhancing your professional duties (e.g., going into the office, bringing work home, studying specific disciplines, working on a certain project, etc.).

While at work, managing your time effectively can be very challenging. There always seems to be some type of an interruption or a distraction of some kind. Whether it is the constant ringing of your phone, a deluge of ad hoc meetings that are being called by your supervisor, constant inquiries from your coworkers about how a software program works or the proverbial "pop in" visit by a close colleague who wants to discuss last night's game with you, they all take up that highly precious and finite resource of yours; your time.

Try visualizing your time as if it were money in your wallet. Consider every hour of your time as one dollar in your wallet, and every fifteen minutes as a quarter. At the start of every new day, visualize your wallet holding $24. As you get out of bed at 6:00 a.m., visualize yourself opening your wallet and immediately discarding the $6 that you "spent" while you were sleeping. After the hour that it takes you to shower, dress and have breakfast, visualize yourself opening that wallet and discarding another $1. After your one-hour commute to work, visualize yourself throwing away another $1. As you sit down at your desk, ready for a fresh day at work, review your to do list for the day and then look into your wallet of time to determine how much time you have left for the day and make sure that you manage those "time dollars" wisely. The person in the aforementioned example had already spent $8 time dollars of their $24 daily allowance on sleeping, showering, dressing and getting to work. Before they even begin their workday, they have already spent 33.3% of their daily time budget. Clearly, I am not saying that you shouldn't sleep, shower or eat breakfast. What I am saying is that you should think of your time as a valuable and finite resource, much like money, and mange it just as wisely as you do your money.

Throughout your workday keep a mental record in your head of how many time dollars you have left to spend before day's end. At noon, if you are working on a high profile project that has a strict deadline and your co-worker asks if you want to try that new restaurant down the road, think to yourself, "It's 12:00, that means I've spent $12 of my $24 time dollars so far for the day and I still have X, Y and Z to do before I leave the office. Do I truly have time for lunch or would my time be better "spent" on something else?" Try spending a couple of days or weeks thinking in these terms and you will develop an natural awareness of how carefully you spend your time.

Prioritizing your work is also critical to spending your time wisely. You should not only keep a written record of all of the tasks, appointments, and projects that need to get done each day, you should also assign a priority level to each of them. This will give you a reference point on what items are most important and what items are not. We all have many things to accomplish throughout the day, some are important and some are not. Some tasks are hard and some tasks are easy. Many of us will routinely focus on the easy tasks first since they can be accomplished and discarded in a relatively short period of time. This gives us a sense of accomplishment; however, procrastinating on the harder tasks will only increase the importance of those tasks further as those pending deadlines draw closer. Therefore, be sure to balance your time each day on both critical and non-critical tasks.

Another important suggestion for assessing how you spend your time is to keep a detailed log of exactly what you do every 15 minutes of the day. Try it for a couple of weeks, including during your personal time. Classify the time you spend by basic categories such as routine assignments, manager-assigned projects, self-assigned projects, self-education, family, leisure, essentials (e.g., sleeping, eating, etc.), etc. Every 15 minutes for a couple of weeks mark down which category your last 15 minutes had fallen into. Assess the results at the end of the trial period. Most people who try this technique are very surprised by the results. Many of us feel as though we are "up to our eyeballs" in work. However, many who try this exercise for some time actually realize that they are only up to their knees in work, but up to their eyeballs with their hobbies, recreational activities, friends, family events and so forth.

Once you have successfully mapped out how you have been spending your time, identify appropriate time wasters and develop an appropriate action plan that addresses the weaknesses in your daily routine. For instance, you might promise yourself not to join that 4:15 gossip gathering each afternoon where immaterial events and issues are discussed ad nausea. If such gatherings typically last until 5:00 or so that means one is wasting $.75 or more than 3.00% of their daily time allowance on such gossip gatherings. You might find that although you feel overworked at the office, it may be because you are leaving work early three days each week to meet your friend at the gym at a certain time. Therefore, you might try asking your friend if you can meet a little later in the evenings, so you can spend an extra 15 to 30 minutes in the office each night closing up your tasks for the day. Be creative when reviewing how you "spend" your time and how you might make better use of your time.

Once you have developed and implemented you own personal time management action plan start tracking how you are spending your time now and compare the results to how you were spending your time before you implemented your action plan. Make sure that you are making progress in terms of devoting time to the appropriate categories.

Never Say, Act or Think…"That's Not My Job"

Corporate America, unlike many manufacturing assembly lines, is not strictly defined by individual job descriptions. Young professionals must clearly have some concept of what their position and roles are within the organization, as well as their individual authorities. However, young professionals must understand that regardless of whether you are an entry level employee, a group supervisor, a division executive or the CEO, you are all working toward a common goal, the success of the organization. As a result, young professionals need to keep an open mind with regards to additional work or assignments that may not fit directly into their specific job description. Technological shortcomings, extraordinary demands due to competitive pressures, human resource and supervisory challenges (e.g., illness, resignations, incompetence, etc.) are unavoidable. In each of these cases, specific individuals may be asked to perform tasks or complete assignments that they are not directly responsible for, all in the interest of the organization. Individuals who can recognize these challenges and adapt their capacities accordingly will position themselves to succeed. Individuals who refuse to contribute additional efforts in the face of such organizational adversity are sure to be labeled as uncommitted and uncooperative, each of which can have calamitous consequences to one's career. Thus, never utter, act or think the words "That is not my job." Rather recognize the problems and challenges not just from your own individual perspective but also from a larger group and organizational perspective and guide your actions accordingly. If you are truly incapable or unable to offer any additional assistance at that particular time, offer your best advice on when and how you might be able to assist in solving the problem. For instance, consider the following two scenarios in which an employee is absent from work, and the group supervisor asks another employee of the group to help cover for the employee who is absent:

Poor Employee Response

> "I know that Mr. Smith [who prepares the monthly project status reports for executive management] is out of the office with an illness, and I do recognize the importance of those reports. However, I am presently in the middle of an urgent project that was assigned to me by Mrs. Thompson [the division executive] who has asked me to complete the project and submit it to her by the end of the week. So, I just don't have time to help. I'm Sorry."

Proper Employee Response

"I recognize that Mr. Smith [who prepares the monthly project status reports for executive management] is out of the office with an illness, and I do recognize the importance of those reports. However, I am presently in the middle of an urgent project that was assigned to me by Mrs. Thompson [the division executive] who has asked me to complete the project and submit it to her by the end of the week. Therefore, I'd be glad to help prepare the monthly project status reports on behalf of Mr. Smith once I complete this project. If this is not an acceptable option, perhaps you [my supervisor] could contact Mrs. Thompson, advise her of this predicament and inquire if she would be agreeable to an extended deadline on the project that I am working on. This would enable me to complete the monthly project status report sooner. What are your thoughts on the matter?

The difference between the poor response and the proper response is that the proper response offers a solution to the problem. Whether the proposed solution is acceptable to the supervisor is actually somewhat irrelevant, the important thing is that the employee does not simply refuse the additional work. The employee in the proper response offers a reasonable solution to the problem, whereas the poor response simply fails to help the supervisor in any way whatsoever. While not specifically stated in the poor response, the employee essentially says, "Sorry, that's not my problem." Not a smart way to try to develop your reputation as a diligent, committed and cooperative member of the group.

Address Others Properly

Until you reach a point in your career where you have developed your political capital, made a favorable reputation for yourself, gained appropriate experiences and built confidence in the eyes of your superiors, you should address your manager and all other senior members of the organization with the proper prefix such as Mr., Mrs., Ms., Dr., etc., until they instruct you not to do so. If your manager truly wants you to refer to him as "John", he will tell you. Until then show your respect for them and their position by addressing them professionally.

Once someone asks you to refer to them by their first name, then feel free to honor their wishes. However, unless a senior member of the organization explicitly tells you to call him or her by their first names, take the high road and stay formal when you address them. This recommendation applies regardless of one's age in relation to the senior member of the organization. For instance, if an employee is older than their manager, the same rule applies. While the employee may in fact be senior in age, the manager is senior in position. Thus, they deserve to be approached with a degree of formality.

The benefits of this cautious approach outweigh the potential drawbacks. A formal approach shows the senior member of the organization that you respect them and their authority. In addition, without knowing much about the senior member, you will not know if they are more of a formal or informal person. Taking the formal approach is the safe bet. If you come across as a bit too casual and comfortable with a senior member of the organization, you run the risk of appearing somewhat overconfident, disrespectful and perhaps even a bit bad mannered. If the senior member is more of an informal person, you still stand to gain, as they will likely view you as a well-mannered and respectful person.

Know Who Your Competition Is

Throughout your entire career, not just in the early stages of your career, you must be aware of exactly who your so-called "competition" is. What I am referring to here is not competition from the perspective of your company, but rather your personal competition in terms of advancement opportunities within the organization. I am referring to internal competition within your company or your department. Exactly, who is it that you will be competing against for that next promotion? Exactly, who is it that you will be competing against for a larger share of the bonus pool? Think of your career as a pyramid, and at its base there are many opportunities to advance early on in your career. As you advance up the corporate ladder, advancement opportunities are less and less available. As you advance to senior and executive level positions, advancement opportunities are even less scarce; thus, competition is typically fiercer as you progress up through the organization.

Each promotional or advancement opportunity that you face, will generally be accompanied by a stiff degree of competition for that position. In many cases, this competition will consist of the very same people that you work with each day. This competition will consist of your co-workers. Given that we spend such a significant part of our life at work, many of us are all too easily drawn into close personal relationships with our co-workers and colleagues. There is nothing necessarily wrong with this, and in fact, you need to develop a strong rapport with your co-workers and colleagues to help strengthen your professional foundation and capacities (e.g., one's reputation, networking abilities, productivity, etc. can all be positively or negatively influence by other members of the group). However, in doing so, you should always remember that these are the people that will likely be competing against you for the next promotional opportunity. Thus, your co-workers must be viewed as your rivalry. Your co-workers are often obstacles to your advancement.

Since you need to maintain a strong rapport with your co-workers, you need to be careful about how you act and perform around them. You need to be careful about what information and experiences you share with them. Be cautious about sharing your ideas and thoughts for improving existing processes or facilities within your department or the organization. You don't want to risk them stealing your ideas. However, do not be recluse or an outsider. Develop these relationships but manage them carefully.

You should also ensure that you preserve the respect from your co-workers, and your own integrity. In other words, do not blatantly sabotage their efforts or maliciously incapacitate them in any way. If they find out that you were behind such efforts, your reputation will be ruined, and you can clearly forget about relying upon them for any assistance or support. Rather, compete against them by out performing, out thinking and out hustling them in any professional way possible. Do the same that they are doing, but do it faster. Do the same that they are doing, but do it better. Do more that they are doing, and do it in less time. Simply try to give a little more than they are giving. For instance, staying later than they do each night is a good example. Knowing more about the industry, marketplace or regulatory environment is another example. Being more involved in corporate functions, fundraisers or other such events is yet another good example. Stay later, speak up, stand out, outshine and know more than your competition, but be careful about acting maliciously or spitefully.

Many of you may find it difficult to think of those who you work with so closely and so personally as your fiercest competition. Many of you may have shared meals, drinks, laughs or tears with these people. However, if you want to be a winner, you need to adopt a winning attitude. To help you adopt such a winning attitude, try visualizing the impact that your competition can have on your life if they advance and you do not. Visualize you and your co-workers competing for one managerial position in the group. If you are married with children, visualize the financial impact this promotional opportunity could have on you and your family. Think about the better vacations that you could take your family on. Think about the expensive holiday gifts that you might be able to purchase for your family members. Think about the better schools or colleges that you might be able to afford for your children. Now, try to visualize if your co-worker were to steal all of that from you. Think about how you would feel if you were literally "robbed" of that promotion. Picture the look on the face of your wife as you tell her that we cannot afford that lavish vacation, picture the looks on the faces of your children as you tell them that you cannot afford those higher priced holiday gifts, think about the greater challenges and obstacles that your children might now have to face by not having the benefit of a better education. How do you feel? Mad? Angry? Motivated? Chances are, all of the above. Now all you have to do is open your eyes and start hustling to make sure that no one in this department or this entire company steals that promotion from you or your family. Use visualization techniques such as this to adopt a winning attitude with your competition.

33

Viewing your co-workers as your toughest competition will ignite a fire within you to reach above and beyond. Viewing your co-workers as your toughest competition will inspire you to do more, do it faster, do it better than anyone else in the company. Quite simply, viewing your co-workers as your toughest competition will drive you and motivate you to be better than they are. In the end, you will win because you will out perform them and recognize your potential. In addition, your company will also win because your efforts will essentially raise the bar for all those that follow in your footsteps, which are seeking such advancement. Others that must advance past you will need to hustle harder than you, which will stimulate greater productivity, greater efficiency, more creativity, etc. You win and your company wins!

Trust Cautiously

Upon your entrance into the wild world of corporate America, you might easily think that you can fully trust some of your close co-workers and colleagues. After all, you will likely be spending more of your waking time with them than your own family. You may have enjoyed each others company at a variety of social events such as happy hour gatherings, weekend getaways to the beach or evening shopping trips to your favorite store. You may easily relate to one another since you may share many of the same duties and responsibilities. You may also commiserate with each other since you may share many of the same frustrations and troubles in the office. However, letting your guard down too early and placing too much trust in someone until they fully prove their allegiance to you can be dangerous. Minute tasks such as asking them for their opinion on a certain topic, asking them to proofread your report or asking them for assistance when you are confronted with an issue of uncertainty can be treacherous territory for you, particularly if you are going to be relying heavily upon their advice. While you may feel as though that you have developed a trusting and dependable relationship with your co-worker, you may be surprised to learn that they may have an ulterior motive such as intentionally misdirecting or misinforming you so as to fabricate your demise; thus, potentially advancing themselves as the group star or standout. As callous as this may sound, it has been known to happen quite frequently, particularly if others view you as a threat to their own career advancement.

Before you place too much trust in your co-workers, offer a small gesture of kindness in some way and see how they respond. If you are caught up on your work, and one of your co-workers is swamped with work, offer to stay late one evening to help them out. If one of your colleagues needs some assistance writing a set of macros for a spreadsheet application that she was asked to create, ask her if she would like you to help. Then, see how they respond to you when your back is against the wall. If you are working late on a time sensitive project, and they offer you nothing more than a quick wave goodnight at 5:00 only three days after you stayed late to help them, this might be a pretty good indication that they are not sincerely interested in assisting you, the same way you assisted them.

So how do you know when you can truly trust someone? While there really is no way of knowing who or when you can truly trust someone, there are certain things that you can do to protect yourself from being overexposed.

Don't jump in headfirst. In other words, your first request for guidance should not pertain to a time sensitive or major project that you were assigned by senior management. Try testing the waters of trust with meaningless or insignificant tasks or issues, which are not likely to have a major impact on your reputation within the group if you are misinformed or misdirected.

Try hedging your bet by secretly asking several of your co-workers for their opinion on the same topic or issue. This will allow you to compare notes and identify any discrepancies in guidance, which are offered. For instance, if you ask four people for their advice on the same topic, and three of them give you the same exact advice, but the fourth one guides you in the completely opposite direction, I would be suspect of that person's advice going forward.

Utilize the relationships that you have developed with some of the long-standing employees in the area to evaluate the integrity and sincerity of others. Simply ask someone who has been around longer than you have, if you can take them out to lunch one day to "pick their brain" on a few things. During lunch ask them some fundamental questions pertaining to your position, the group or the organization. However, while doing so, surreptitiously inquire about the individual(s) you are evaluating for trustworthiness. Don't invite them to lunch just to ask questions about other people, this appears callous and ruthless on your part; therefore, you need to be prepared to ask some basic questions pertaining to other subjects. Ask them how skilled and knowledgeable they think the others are? Ask them if they consider the others to be truly sincere and compassionate about helping others? This is a great way to get the scoop on other members of the group, just be cautious about being too obvious about it. In other words, try couching your inquisitions within the context of a relevant discussion. For instance, "I was in the office late last night closing up the Thompson Project and Sam really helped me out with the MIS reporting on the project. He really seems like a big help around here, wouldn't you agree?"

Never Talk Money

Amongst the most sacred rules in corporate America is to never talk about your salary or bonus. It is unprofessional to do so and can lead to absolutely no good. You might think that you can truly trust your close colleagues or friends at the office with such information, and you may feel an obligation to reciprocate if they tell you how much they are making; however, never divulge this information to anyone who works in your company. If you share this information with a trusted colleague of yours who happens to hold a similar position in the company and you are earning more than they are, they are more than likely going to be upset. Your so-called "trusted colleague" could very easily turn into a not so trusted colleague. Furthermore, they may start gossiping to other coworkers about your compensation, many of whom you might not trust, and many of whom may actually be out to plan your demise (so they can get ahead themselves). If your coworkers are aware of your compensation and are jealous of your compensation, they are much less likely to assist you when you need help, guidance or advice of any kind. In other words, you run a serious and potentially catastrophic risk of jeopardizing many key relationships within the company if you choose to divulge your compensation. You run the risk of sabotaging your own potential to advance by upsetting many of the people whom you may rely upon to help you do your job, build political capital and develop a favorable reputation.

Additionally, if your manager or the human resources department learns that your compensation is known by others, and that this has led to a decline in morale for the group, I would venture a guess that your manager is going to be red hot mad. They will be mad at you for not having the common sense and professional etiquette to keep your compensation to yourself. Moreover, your manager will now have to deal with a group of frustrated, angry, morale deflated and probably unproductive staff members, all thanks to your decision to share your compensation with that so called trusted colleague. I can assure you that if you ever place your manager in a position like this, they will certainly never forget it.

Some of you may be asking "Well what if my co-worker tells me what their compensation is, and I learn that he or she earns more than me for doing the same job, shouldn't I be upset?" The answer is yes; however, the manner in which you handle it should be professional, deliberate and well planned out. If you determine that other co-workers are earning more than you for doing the same job, before your approach your manager about your compensation, be sure that your higher paid colleagues have similar educational backgrounds, professional experiences, talents and performance records as you. In other words, if you and your co-workers are both junior accountants, and you are informed by your co-worker that she is making 15% more than you in salary, determine what her education and professional experiences are and compare them to yours. If your co-worker has earned her MBA, and you have not; while you may in fact hold the same position within the company, are your education levels truly similar? No. If your co-worker had worked for a separate accounting firm for three years prior to joining your company, and you were hired straight out of college are your professional experiences truly similar? No. Make sure that your co-workers education and professional experiences are truly similar to yours.

If you do determine that your co-worker is earning more than you and has a truly similar educational background as you, has similar professional experiences as you, has similar talents and a similar performance record as you, consider how you are going to handle the situation. Do not take any sudden action and do not let your manager know that you are aware what you co-worker's salary is. This could damage your relationship with that co-worker and could also adversely affect your reputation with others in the group who might perceive you as a "tattle-tale." Rather, if you find yourself in a situation where you are disappointed at your level of compensation relative to others in the group who hold similar positions, and hold similar educational and professional backgrounds, pledge to yourself that you will not take any action for at least one or two weeks. That way, you will prevent yourself from acting solely upon sheer emotions and will assure yourself sufficient time to think about how you want to handle the matter. Take the time to think about what you want to say to your manager and how you will say it. Take the time to present a case for yourself. Build your argument by preparing a list of extra work that you have completed, additional tasks that you have accomplished, important deadlines that have been met, key contributions that you have made, cite specific examples of the times where you have gone above and beyond the call of duty (e.g., coming in on weekends, staying late into the evenings to finish an important assignment, etc.).

If you feel as though your position is under paid compared to similar positions at other companies in the same area, do some homework ahead of time and cite what those positions are paying and what you are being paid. There are many job searching websites out on the internet that reference starting salary information that might assist you with this. There are also many salary survey websites that may help. In presenting your case however, be sure to stress you desire to stay at your current employer, stress the pleasure you have in working for your manager, stress the gratitude you have to them for training and developing you and stress the fact that you honestly want to work for an organization where you can grow some roots, develop your talent and contribute to the corporate mission. However, at the same time, stress your desire to be compensated fairly for your efforts. Your chances of success are greatly improved if you take the diplomatic and politically correct approach with your manager and support your claims with concrete facts, rather than storming into their office and simply demanding a raise.

In closing, keep in mind that asking your manager for a raise is not something that should be done regularly, if ever. Therefore, be selective about when you choose to approach them with such a request. You cannot be expected to request such compensatory adjustments too regularly, or you will be perceived poorly, so plan your efforts carefully.

Key points to remember are as follows:

- NEVER discuss your compensation with anyone in your company. You never truly know whom you can trust.

- You run a serious risk of jeopardizing key relationships within the company if you do divulge your compensation.

- If you learn that you coworkers are earning more than you, do not let your manager know that you know what your co-worker is making and do not take any action for some time. This will prevent you from being guided by emotion and will allow you some time to do some research and plan an appropriate strategy.
    - Ask yourself are the educations, professional experiences, talents and performance records of my co-worker and I truly comparable.
    - Build your argument by preparing a list of extra work that you have completed, additional tasks that you have accomplished, important deadlines that have been met, key contributions that you have made, cite specific examples of the times where you have gone above and beyond the call of duty (e.g., coming in on weekends, etc.), etc.
    - Survey salaries for similar positions at competing companies in the same area.
    - Stress your pleasure at working for your manager and working at your employer, but stress your desire, in a polite,

professional and respectable manner to be compensated fairly for your efforts.

- Requests for raises, no matter how diplomatic and well planned they may be, should not be done too regularly.

Ask For Help, When Necessary

When you are confronted with an unfamiliar situation, do not be afraid to seek the assistance of your co-workers, colleagues or your manager. Many young professionals view asking for help as an act of incompetence, and are therefore hesitant to seek advice or guidance. However, seeking advice on a situation, after you have exhausted all other reasonable efforts (e.g., reviewed company policies and procedures, performed due diligence and research, etc.), shows that you take your responsibilities seriously and are concerned about proceeding properly.

Young professionals should not be intimidated or hesitant to approach senior members of their department or their manager for guidance, but they should understand that these individuals do have roles and responsibilities to fulfill themselves. Therefore, efforts should be made to make this process as efficient and easy as possible for the person giving you direction.

Among the first things to understand are the resources that are available to assist you. If you have a policy and procedure manual or some other form of reference material that may benefit you, the best advice is to closely review this information first. If you are still uncertain and unsure how to proceed, there is nothing wrong with asking for some help.

If you have developed an appropriate relationship with some senior members of your department and you have developed a sense of trust with them, you might try seeking their advice first, before seeking advice from your manager. However, in some cases managers may not encourage this and would rather the young professional seek advice directly from the manager. Upon your hire, ask your manager whom you should seek advice from when needed. Ask if they would like you to seek their advice exclusively or, in the interest of making their jobs easier, whether they have any objection to you soliciting advice and guidance from other members of the department first before approaching you. If they have no such objection to you seeking advice from other members of the department, ask if there are any particular members that they would prefer you go to for advice.

Regardless of who you are seeking advice from, follow these rules:

- Ask the person if you could meet with them to discuss an issue that you are not quite clear on, and try to estimate how much time you will need. This will enable them to gauge whether they have time for your question now or if you should come back at a later time. For instance, be sure to let your helper know if you need 5 minutes or 1 hour of their time.

- Assemble relevant questions in "clusters" rather than peppering the person with various questions throughout the day or week. This will minimize the downtime of the person offering you advice and direction.

- Be prepared. This will prevent unnecessary delays in the meeting.
  - Have any and all supporting information (e.g., files, documentation, figures, source data, etc.) concerning that issue with you at the meeting. This way you are prepared if the person offering you advice requires additional information to answer your question(s) or needs to review the supporting materially personally.
  - If you are reviewing a specific document, have copies prepared ahead of time for all members in the meeting.
  - Before getting into the specific details of the obstacle, set the stage of your dilemma for the person offering you advice and direction. Discuss the context of your challenge (e.g., what you are trying to accomplish, what purpose your task is serving, etc.). This will help the person determine if you are essentially on the right track or if you are way off target.

- Before concluding the meeting, be sure that you understand the answer or direction that was provided to you. If you do not comprehend what was told to you, you may likely need to seek advice on the issue again. If necessary, tell the person offering you advice that you are truly interested in understanding the intricacies of this issue, but that you are having some difficulty comprehending the nature of the solution or advice. Be specific about what it is that you are having difficulty understanding, so that they can focus their efforts on that issue in particular.

- At the end of the meeting, be sure to thank them for their time and efforts in assisting you.

Do Not Over Use Email

Email is an extraordinary tool that has helped accelerate the overall pace of business not just in corporate America, but throughout the global marketplace. Email has improved efficiencies and enhanced access to information. It seems almost archaic to think of the days before email. Today's young professionals are much more exposed to email, text messaging, cell phones and other communication enhancers than some of their senior counterparts. Such other forms of communication can be considered somewhat impersonal and include email, text messaging, instant messaging, interactions through social networking websites, and so forth. Many young people who were accustomed to these types of communication vehicles throughout their entire high school, college and young adult years have developed, what I would say is a dangerous dependence on these types of communications. So much so, that some might reasonably argue that opportunities to develop certain fundamental interpersonal and social networking skills have been severely restricted for these individuals. Why speak to someone personally when I can just send them a text message? Why meet with someone personally, when I can just email the information that they need?

Young professionals who were raised on these types of communication vehicles throughout much of their lives appear to rely much more heavily on these communication methods, particularly when it concerns a subject or issue that they are not fully confident of or knowledgeable about. Perhaps they use email as a shield to protect them from spontaneous inquisitions from their target audience. Perhaps they use email to avoid confrontations with short-tempered managers or clients. Perhaps they use email because they have not fully developed their communication, presentation or public speaking skills. Whatever the case may be, overuse of email, and other such forms of communication is not proper office etiquette and will not help to develop the employee's interpersonal skills, which are essential to one's success. To help you better under when NOT to use email, follow these tips.

Never use email when:

- You are seeking an "active" back and forth dialogue on an issue.

- You are simply trying to avoid a confrontation or inquisition of some kind.

- Your message is sensitive, personal or confidential.

- Your message might be misunderstood or viewed as somewhat ambiguous.

- You have never met or spoken with the intended person before. First encounters should be face to face or made via the telephone.

- You are angry or when you are strategically interested in conveying a specific feeling in your message (e.g., happiness, gratitude, sympathy, anger, etc.). Instead, pick up the phone and speak to the respective party in person or meet with them personally.

Save The Sick Time

While an employee may be fully entitled to a certain number of sick days each year, they should never use their full allotment, or anywhere near it, unless absolutely necessary. Many employees seem to believe that since they are "entitled" to such sick time, that they are free to use all such time, regardless of how sick or healthy they may be, with no adverse ramifications to their career. However, employees regardless of how junior or senior their positions must understand that sick time is intended solely for that purpose, and its abuse can in fact have adverse ramifications on how an employee is viewed in the eyes of their manager.

Sick time should only be used when an employee is incapacitated with a contagious or serious illness that restricts them from performing their day-to-day responsibilities at work. Sick time is not intended to be an extension of one's allotted vacation time. There is a common perception among many managers that employees who routinely utilize all of their allotted sick time each year are perhaps abusing the privilege of their duly allotted sick time. An employee who routinely utilizes all of their allotted sick time is often perceived as having a "clock watching" attitude, someone who is more interested in what the company is giving them rather than what they are giving the company. Such employees are often viewed as individuals interested in meeting only the bare minimum in terms of expected performance. In other words, these employees are often viewed as those who routinely show up for work exactly at 9:00 and leave the office exactly at 5:00. These employees are not typically viewed as those with strong work ethics willing to go above and beyond standard expectations.

Clearly if you are truly incapacitated with a serious illness and need to take a leave from work, you should do so; however, when calling in sick, follow this advice:

- Always speak with your manager directly when calling in. Employees are often afraid to speak to their manager when calling in sick. Many will leave a voice mail with their manager early in the morning when they know that their manager is not at their desk. Speaking directly with your manager adds credibility to the employee's claim that they are truly and seriously ill. Leaving a voicemail when the employee knows full well that their manager is not at their desk is the easy way out and often viewed with a degree of skepticism by the manager.

- If you are out sick for more than one business day, call your manager each morning to update them on your condition and your expectations on your return to work.

- Brief your manager on any pending items you are working on. Also, by speaking with your manager directly, you will be able to inform them of any important projects or tasks that need to be completed while you are out. This will allow the manager to reassign any necessary work, if needed.

- Leave your phone number and email. While your manager probably has your home phone number or personal cell number, offer it to them again and tell them that they are welcome to call you if they need you for anything. Offering this information exhibits professionalism and illustrates a commitment to your work even when you are not capable of coming into the office.

- Upon your return to work, consider taking the time off as vacation time instead. While I recognize that this can be a serious personal sacrifice, such a tactic will help to preserve your reputation as a committed and loyal employee.

- Apologize to your manager for the absence and offer to catch up on any unfinished work by coming in earlier, staying later or coming in on weekends. Regardless of whether or not your manager takes you up on your offer, the mere offer will serve you well in the eyes of your manager.

Do Not Date Your Co-Workers

As a young professional just starting out on your career, it is quite possible that you may find yourself in the midst of some office romance. The daily environment of a young professional is often rather conducive to such romance. Young professionals are often single. Young professionals are likely working with many other individuals of similar age and background. Young professionals often work together for many hours at a time on special projects, tasks or assignments. Such work often stretches beyond the standard working hours and may extend late into the evenings or the weekends. Young professionals who are working together are likely to share many things in common (e.g., your educational background, your employer, your supervisor, etc.), and you are likely to turn to each other when in need of assistance, support or simply someone to vent your frustrations on. Young professionals are also likely to share an occasional drink or two during an office happy hour or corporate function. However, dating your co-workers can be dangerous and can taint your reputation as a professional if you are not careful.

Dating someone you work with might seem relatively harmless at the time; however, in the event things go sour between the two of you, some may find it difficult to continue a productive working relationship together. For the most part senior management, and your employer, do not care about your personal life or what you chose to do with your own personal time; however, while you are on company time and on company property, they expect you to act like a true professional, to conduct yourself appropriately and to be able to perform at you best, no matter who it is that you are working with, period!

In addition to the no dating rule, you should also restrict yourself from flirting and expressing other forms of affection towards your co-workers. Even though you may have no intention of actually dating them, and see no harm in an occasional flirt, it is quite possible that your boss or senior management may view you as somewhat distracted and incapable of working seriously with an attractive member of the opposite sex.

Best advice here is to keep it strictly business-related when dealing with your co-workers.

Sign Off

Never submit a memorandum, letter of any other form of correspondence to your boss or senior member of the company without your signature or initials. In fact, many managers will simply refuse to review any document from an employee that lacks their signature. Your signature signifies that you are taking responsibility for the content and accuracy of the information contained in the document and that you fully support its statements, findings and conclusions. If you are not fully confident of the accuracy or the thoroughness of the document, you should not be submitting it to your boss. In such situations, leverage the value of the rapport that you have developed with your co-workers, colleagues and mentors to assist you in ensuring the accuracy of your document. This will relieve some of the burden on your boss and presumably make their job somewhat easier. Young professionals today must recognize and respect the hectic schedules of their bosses. Managers simply cannot be expected to review a document that the author is not fully confident of. While it is fully recognized that many submissions by young professionals will in fact be wrong, inaccurate or insufficient in detail, the onus and burden of ensuring that the document is suitable must fall squarely on the shoulders of the author, not the reviewer. All too often, young professionals will simply give up on a task and knowingly submit an inadequate document with the expectation that their bosses will fix their mistakes or correct their data. This is inappropriate and totally unacceptable. Young professionals have to be accountable for their work and make all reasonable attempts to ensure that the document is accurate and sufficient before submitting it to their boss. If errors or inaccuracies are found, it should not be from a lack of effort on behalf of the author.

With regard to submitting a document or memorandum by way of email, do not send your email until you are fully satisfied with the document's content. In terms of corporate etiquette, the action of sending an email to your boss is no different that submitting a document to he or she with your written signature or initials. As such, when sending an email to your boss or any other senior member of the company, be sure that you fully support its content.

Seek Feedback From Your Boss

Many of you may have heard the saying "You never know, unless you ask." When it comes to seeking feedback from your boss regarding your performance and future growth opportunities, this statement is resoundingly true. This can often be a significant failing among many of today's young professionals. Many think, "as long as I work hard, and do well, I will advance." However, it is sad to state that many managers and bosses are oblivious to the individual aspirations and expectations of their employees. Furthermore, many of today's young professionals are either scared or uncomfortable approaching their managers and soliciting their opinion about their performance and their opportunities for advancement.

Most companies do require annual performance evaluations, and some may require them more often. Unfortunately, many managers often fail to take full advantage of these opportunities. These evaluations are designed to give specific feedback to the employee about their performance, their weaknesses, their expectations for future performance, their objectives for the next year, etc. Unfortunately, many managers view these evaluations as a burdensome mandate from the company's human resource group rather than a critical growth and development tool for the employee. Thus, efforts to complete such evaluations are often limited, feedback offered is often vague and the value of the evaluation to the employee is often restricted. Moreover, the all to common "annual" performance evaluation is often grossly insufficient to truly guide and develop a young professional. Young professionals need to know on a much more regular basis how they are doing and what they need to improve upon.

This inattentiveness to employees needs and the failure to properly prepare and execute employees' performance evaluations can often stall one's advancement. This coupled with the reluctance of many young professionals to approach their managers more regularly and seek their specific advice and guidance can prohibit them from receiving valuable information about how they are performing, what they need to improve upon, what is expected of them in the future and where they can expect to go in the organization if such expectations are met.

If you are starting a new job or a new position, wait until you have had sufficient time to "learn the ropes" of the position. Once this has occurred, and you are satisfied with your day-to-day performance, approach your boss and ask if he or she could spend a few minutes with you talking about your performance and your growth and development opportunities. Ask your manager if you could set a date and time in the near future for this meeting. If they have time right then and there for you, it's best if you politely suggest a future date and time to meet. This will allow your manager some time to prepare for the meeting, review your file, your work, etc. This will ensure that the guidance that you receive from your manager is based upon well-prepared and well thought out information. Be proactive and take the initiative to start a dialogue about your performance. When you are requesting such a meeting, be specific about what it is that you wish to speak about. Tell them that you would like to ask them how you are doing, what you need to do better and what you need to accomplish in order to advance to the next position. Ask them to be honest and frank. Suggest that they offer you sincere and genuine constructive criticism. Let your boss know that you are not looking for a feel good "keep up the good work!" type meeting; you are looking for tangible advice that you can use to improve yourself as a professional.

During this initial meeting, explain to your manager that you are interested in their opinion and guidance as it relates to your performance. Explain that, in addition to the formal performance evaluations, you would appreciate more regular meetings with them to gauge your performance against established expectations. Explain to them that you feel that this will not only benefit you as a professional, but the group as a whole, and thus your manager as well. You may also wish to review with your manager your one, three and five year career plans. Ask them if they feel your career plans are fair and reasonable. If not, ask them why. The frequency of these meetings should be no less than semi annual but no more than monthly. Any less than two meetings per year will not provide you with sufficient oversight and guidance to direct your progress. Meetings more frequent than once per month may become too burdensome to your manager, which could adversely affect the effectiveness of the meetings.

During these meetings be specific with them when asking questions, such as "What is my biggest weakest?, How can I improve upon it?". Ask them where they see you fitting into the organization 1, 3 and 5 years down the road? This shows that you are proactive about developing yourself and illustrates your desire to advance.

Be sure to keep a written record of these meetings, what was discussed, what expectations were established, what objectives were achieved, what action plans were set, etc. The next time that you meet with your manager, discuss exactly what you have done since the last meeting to meet their expectations. If you have continually met your manager's expectations and achieved those objectives that were set for you, and you still have not advanced to greater opportunities within the organization, inquire to your manager why not.

A regular dialogue with your manager is a critical tool in helping you to gauge your performance, identify weaknesses, establish appropriate objectives, develop meaningful action plans, all of which will further your professional development and ultimately assist you in advancing yourself to greater opportunities.

Think In Terms Of Solutions, Not Problems

Throughout your entire career, you will encounter challenges, problems and obstacles. Given the no nonsense rapid fire pace of corporate culture today, such difficulties must be dealt with in a prompt fashion. In your continuous desire to build a stronger and stronger reputation for yourself, and in your continuous desire to develop your own political capital, you should never simply present a problem to your manager and seek their guidance. You must first identify the problem, identify all possible and/or reasonable solutions, evaluate all possible solutions and ultimately decide upon the most appropriate course of action. Finally, you should then ask for your manager's opinion as to your recommendation. Consider the following two scenarios:

Scenario 1
"Excuse me, Mr. Manager. As I was reviewing the collateral file, I noticed that the legal documents for ABC Co. were not properly executed and were not originals. How would you like me to handle this?"

Scenario 2
"Excuse me, Mr. Manager. As I was reviewing the collateral file, I noticed that the legal documents for ABC Co. were not properly executed and were not originals. I presumed that the documents could be in one of three locations. They might have accidentally been sent to the client, they might be with the account officer in his desk file or they might still be with our legal department. I didn't think we wanted to contact our client, without checking internally first so I just checked with the paralegal, who said that she sent the documents to the account officer. I contacted the account officer myself. He had someone in his office, but briefly checked his files, and seems to think he might have accidentally sent the original documents to the client instead of the copies. I would be happy to contact the client myself. However, given the long standing relationship between the client and the account officer, I would first suggest that the account officer take a second and more thorough look through his office and if he still cannot find the documents, than I would recommend that he contact the client himself so as to maintain the integrity of the relationship. If you agree, I'll be happy to call the account officer and advise him of the situation. If not, how would suggest I handle the situation?"

Presenting the problem, reviewing all of the potential solutions and recommending what you feel is the most appropriate solutions shows your manager that you are not simply "bailing out" of the problem. It shows your manager that you are capable of (1) identifying problems, (2) reviewing all of the potential solutions, (3) evaluating all solutions based upon the current environment and circumstances and ultimately (3) deciding what the most appropriate course of action is. Regardless of whether your manager chooses to agree with your recommendation, these efforts illustrate two of the most critical ingredients in most any professional position, critical thinking and problem-solving skills.

Own Up To Your Mistakes

When you are placed in a position of having to answer to a senior member of the organization about an error, oversight or deficiency that you were responsible for or played a role in, do not just apologize for the error and indicate that you will fix it. Doing so can easily be construed by someone as dispassionate or unconcerned about the issue. Rather, you need to take responsibility and build back the confidences that may have been lost in you as a result of the error. To help you do this, try adhering to the following six-steps when you must own up to a mistake:

1. Apologize for the error and its subsequent inconvenience that it may have caused anyone,

2. Acknowledge the problem and take responsibility (accountability) for it,

3. Express your understanding of how significant the error is and its implications,

4. Indicate that you will promptly fix the problem,

5. In a follow up phone call, email, memo or meeting, convey your "ownership" of the issue, by committing to research and implement a proper control or procedure (no matter how sophisticated or unsophisticated) to ensure that it doesn't happen again. In other words, be sure that you learn from your mistakes and never repeat the same mistake twice.

6. Most of all, NEVER MAKE EXCUSES! Managers don't really care why the error occurred. Managers only know that an error was made and they want to feel confident that it will never happen again.

Consider the following two scenarios:

Your manager storms into your cubicle, throws down a report that you had prepared for him or her (which was ultimately sent to senior and executive management for their review as well), screaming and yelling at you because the report contained a glaring mathematical error.

Uninterested and Dispassionate Response
"I'm sorry. I must have been too pre-occupied with the other task that you assigned me this morning. I'll fix it right away."

Committed and Passionate Response
"Let me apologize for the error as well as the inconveniences it has caused you and senior management. Please be aware that I take full and complete responsibility for this oversight and fully recognize the seriousness of it. I want you to know that I recognize the importance of this data and understand that you and senior management rely upon this information to make certain strategic decisions. Last, let me ensure you that I will see to it that this error is fixed immediately, and that proper controls are established to prevent similar errors from ever occurring again."

Later on, after the smoke has cleared a little, in a follow up email to his manager, the employee sends the following message:

"I wanted to take this opportunity to reiterate my apologies for the error that was identified in the monthly sales report. Given the severity of this data, and the importance of this data in assisting you with your responsibilities, I wanted to ensure that this error does not reoccur. Therefore, effective immediately, I am developing and implementing the following controls:

1. I intend on starting the data gathering process earlier in the month to allow more time to review and input the appropriate information into the report. I have already installed an automatic reminder alarm on my scheduling application concerning this task

2. I have created a computer spreadsheet file with imbedded mathematical formulas, which are password protected so as to prevent their modification, which will automatically perform the necessary calculations.

3. I am fully committing myself to proofing all data contained in the report before submitting the report to you.

I am fully confident that these steps will prevent this error from recurring.

Thank you."

Stay Calm

Regardless of whether you are a young professional or a seasoned professional, at many times throughout your career you are likely to encounter a significant amount of stress, pressure and frustration while performing your duties and responsibilities. The high stakes associated with corporate on-goings (e.g., profits, bonuses, promotions, etc.), the reputations that are on the line when tasks are completed incorrectly or not on time, the constant power plays between various members of an organization and the various personalities at play will eventually cause most of us to lose our cool at some point. It is not a question of "If", it is a question of "When" and it is a question of "How" we respond in such situations.

Many of us have seen it first hand, and many of us have heard true horror stories of employees losing control of their emotions at work ultimately resulting in a variety of actions ranging from crying, screaming, name calling, keyboard banging, fist pounding, door slamming, object throwing, paper ripping, spreadsheet crumpling, and so forth. You also have the many passive-aggressive behaviors such as intended unresponsiveness, heavy sighing or eye rolling that many choose to utilize.

Let me just say that it is considered acceptable to raise your voice on occasion and vent your frustration; however, be exceptionally careful about whom it is directed at, how it might be perceived by others and how often it happens. First, never get personal; always remain professional and dignified in your behavior. Second, if you are venting "up" (meaning, up the chain of command) be darn sure that your facts are straight, your homework is done and that you know exactly what it is that you are talking about. Third, do not let it happen too often. Nonetheless, this type of a display once in a while shows people that you are truly passionate about your work and that you take your responsibilities seriously.

Regardless of the underlying circumstances behind the situation, regardless of how trivial or significant the matter, as a young professional it is important that you retain your composure and not lose your temper. This can be difficult for many young professionals, as they might not have had sufficient experience in working under such difficult conditions. Staying calm in the face of adversity is an important quality in senior management. Staying calm under such duress is essential as it allows you to focus on the problem at hand and develop an appropriate solution.

Allowing your emotions to get in the way of your thought process will only inhibit your productivity, efficiency and effectiveness. By maintaining your composure in the face of adversity, you are conveying the message that you are in control of your emotions, in command of the matter and capable of reasoning through all possible alternatives to develop a valuable solution.

It is recognized that many managers and executives rule their employees with an iron fist, often screaming and yelling at them as a means of motivating them. Regardless of whether you agree or disagree about the modern day effectiveness of this particular style of management, it does occur quite often and employees need to know how to handle these situations. As a young professional seeking to be viewed as a competent, capable and controlled you must not deviate from a calm and collected disposition. As a young professional you have to maintain your cool.

Consider for a moment a young police officer taking cover behind a small car as he is caught in the middle of a fierce firefight with armed robbers. Until backup arrives, the safety and well being of this police officer hinges greatly upon his ability to control his emotions, think clearly, consider all potential alternatives and decide upon the most appropriate course of action. This cannot be done effectively unless he controls his emotions and maintains his composure. While the stakes may be vastly different, the scenario itself runs parallel to the many challenges often confronting millions of employees in corporate America every day. To be successful, employees in any position of uncertainty, adversity or anxiety must be successful at controlling themselves and their emotions.

Step Quickly and Stand Straight

Anyone who has ever worked in an office setting probably knows what I am talking about here. There are those people who slowly and casually move around the office as if they have all the time in the world to get to where they are going, and there are those who move around the office swiftly with purpose and vigor. Regardless of whether you are on your way to a Board meeting or whether you are on your way to the cafeteria, the way you carry yourself and the pace at which you move, can influence how others perceive you and your work ethic. A young professional may not have anywhere to go, or anything important to do at a particular moment, but the manner in which they move can send dramatically different messages to those around them. The actions of the casual slow mover basically screams, "I have nothing important to do, nowhere to go, and I'm in no hurry to do anything of value." The person who strides around the office with a noticeable spring in their step says "I've got somewhere to be, I've got something important to do, and I have to do it now, so please excuse me." The mere pace at which someone walks around the office can, and often is, a reflection of his or her own individual work ethic. The lack of urgency associated with the casual slow mover sends a message and a vibe that they are not busy and not working on anything important. The quick stepping employee sends a message and a vibe that they recognize the importance of their duties, that they are a go-getter, a hustler and someone who is interested in contributing some value to the organization.

In addition to the pace at which people walk around the office, there are other signs such as slumped shoulders, a lowered head, and poor eye contact that can send negative messages to your managers and senior management. Others can often interpret poor body posture as a lack of self-confidence and lack of self-assurance in one's abilities. How do you expect others to believe in your knowledge, work ethic, competence and value to the organization, if you do not appear as though you are fully confident of your own talent and capacities? Therefore, in addition to making sure that you step quickly and purposefully around the office, be sure to stand straight, keep your shoulders back and chin up so as to facilitate an appropriate image of purpose and confidence to those around you.

Learn How To Make An Impression

Meeting someone for the first time will often leave a lasting impression. Whether this impression is positive or negative is completely up to you. A poor first impression can adversely affect how someone thinks of you as a professional, and what's worse is that these first impressions can be difficult to correct or change. Thus, it is critical that you understand the proper etiquette of professional encounters. I suggest the following tips to help you successfully handle such situations:

Stand Up – If you are seated when someone approaches you with an introduction, stand up to greet the person(s). This simple act shows a tremendous amount of respect and courtesy toward the person and lets them know that you are willing to stop what you are doing in order to give them your full attention.

Make Eye Contact - Looking the person in their eyes shows a degree of confidence on your part. It also shows them respect and lets them know that you are truly listening to them and attentive to their presence.

Shake Firmly - When shaking hands with anyone, offer them a firm handshake making sure to grasp their entire hand, not just their fingers. A solid and firm handshake is often correlated to a sense of confidence and assurance. Anyone who has shook hands with a firm shaker knows what I am referring to. On the contrary, anyone who has been on the receiving end of the proverbial "wet noodle" handshake also knows what I am talking about. Those of us who have received a soft, gentle, fingertip shake from someone who fails to make eye contact with us will often view that person as shy and reclusive, and thus somewhat unsure of themselves and their abilities.

Be Excited - Show excitement when meeting someone. Showing excitement in meeting someone, particularly a senior member of the organization is a display of respect for that person's position and authority. A good way of doing this is simply offering a warm and welcoming smile and a rather generic yet very effective "Hello, Mr. Smith, it's a pleasure to meet you." This will immediately disarm your partner and let them know that you are sincerely pleased to meet them.

Use Their Name - Use the person's name both when you are first introduced and when concluding the encounter. For instance, "It's a pleasure to meet you Mr. Smith" and "Have a great day Mr. Smith." A person's name is amongst their most sacred possessions. Using the person's name in the beginning and ending of a conversation lets your partner know that you were listening to the introduction and made a mental note of who they are.

Say Something - When meeting a senior member of the company, it is important that you offer a welcoming statement other than a curt and simple "Hello." Expand your introduction and let them know how excited you are to meet them. For instance: "Hello Mr. Smith, it is a pleasure to meet you. You know I have to tell you how excited I am to be working here." However, it is equally important that you not get too conversational (unless your senior partner engages you first in the conversation). Senior managers are generally very busy and typically cannot be bothered with extended conversations with employees whom they are not overly involved with. In other words, most senior managers do not have the time or the patience to spend 30 minutes with you as they listen to you recite your entire educational background and professional experiences. Make a statement, but keep it brief.

Lose The Street Language

As a college student, you might not have realized it since many of your peers were probably speaking the same way. However, it is possible that you, and most of your peers may have developed a style and manner of speaking that might not be entirely appropriate for the office or fully understood by some of your fellow co-workers and colleagues. You may have developed a habit of using certain words, terms or phrases that might not necessarily be fully recognized by senior members of your employer, namely your manager, senior management or your clients.

I'm not referring to the use of foul or inappropriate language, which should be used very sparingly, if ever in the office. Here I am referring to the use of street jargon and slang. Words such as "tight", "sweet", "phat", etc. are all relatively inoffensive, but not necessarily representative of how senior management might want an up and coming young professional to speak routinely in the office, and certainly to clients. I can recall the first time I shared a certain story with a young professional in the office. The ending of the story had a considerable degree of surprise to it, to which the young man replied, "shut up!" I was taken aback for a moment, as I thought he meant that I should literally shut up. However, I soon realized that this was said in sort of an incredulous and humorous manner, and not meant in literal terms.

I am also referring to the manner in which certain words, terms or phrases are spoken. In other words, try to use proper pronunciation. For instance, when answering someone affirmatively, say "yes" not "yeah." When answering negatively, say "no" not "Nah." When someone greets you in the morning say "Good morning" not "What's up?" When someone says good night to you say "Good Night" not "Later!"

Additionally, be mindful of how often you use words such as "like" in your speech. For whatever reason, words such as "like" appear to have found a pronounced role in the speech of many of today's recent college graduates and young professionals. Again, while there may not necessarily be anything wrong with the use of this word in your daily speech, over use of the word, is not consistent with proper speaking and not consistent with the image that you are trying to convey, which is an educated, knowledgeable and skilled professional.

Speaking appropriately by not using jargon or slang and using proper pronunciation will go a long way to creating a favorable impression and a professional image within the organization. Ideally, this favorable impression and professional image will make it easier for your manager or senior management to visualize you in a position with greater responsibility, greater exposure to senior management or greater exposure to valued clients, each of which will ultimately assist in your advancement throughout the organization.

Keep A Busy Work Space

During an interview or a meeting, have you ever noticed how someone's desk and office is kept? For a moment, just imagine a desk free of all but one or two sheets of paper, with the only other object being a perfectly straightened pen and pencil set. Now imagine a desk awash in a sea of files, reports, memos, letters and so forth. If I were to ask you, which employee "appears" busier, what would you say? I did not ask you which employee is "truly" busier. While it may not be fair to judge someone's productivity or capabilities on the manner in which their desk or office is kept, it is possible that people are in fact quite often judged on such things. Similarly, imagine two employees walking out of the building. One has absolutely nothing in his hands other than his car keys as he casually strolls out of the building gently whistling the tune to a popular TV program. The other employee has a bulging briefcase in one hand, a set of files in the other hand, his car keys dangling from his little finger, and a cell phone pinned to his ear. If you had to guess, whom do you think will be perceived as the "busier" employee? Again, just because someone has a full briefcase and is carrying a set of files does not mean that they are in fact any more busy than the other employee with nothing in their hands. However, you must understand that there are those who may quite easily form opinions of you on such things. Therefore, it is recommended that you keep a busy looking desk and workspace to prevent people from forming an opinion of you that it not productive and diligent.

Allow me to make a point here, busy looking does not mean cluttered and messy, and it certainly does not mean disorganized. You should have pertinent materials available and visible to you and any of your visitors, which may be relevant to your day-to-day duties and responsibilities. Do not hide all these materials away and out of sight. Make them visible for people to see on your desk or in your cubicle or office. Also, be sure that you know where everything is on your desk. Have a system where everything is placed, so items can be easily retrieved when needed.

A busy workspace conveys a sense of diligence and industriousness. It also conveys a message about your ability to handle multiple tasks. Having multiple files, reports, etc. on your desk appears that you are working on various tasks, all at once. Having little on your desk appears as though you are in fact working on a little. The ultimate idea is to create and display a workspace that attempts to illustrate your capacities and abilities as a hard-working and fully capable employee.

Do Not Play Music At The Office

Playing some low volume music in the confines of your own cubicle may sound like a rather harmless act that one may reasonably argue may actually act as a practical tension reliever and stress reducer; however, in your effort to be perceived and treated as a true professional, you should strive to act like a true professional. As a young professional seeking to develop meaningful relationships and create positive standing within the organization this one simple act could actually serve to disturb, annoy and agitate other members of your area, other members of your area whom you may come to rely upon to help you complete a major assignment or large project. While the soft sounds of your favorite group may be soothing and comforting to your ears, the same might not be the case for others.

Moreover, even if you and all of your localized co-workers happen to agree that your music is enjoyable, you do not want to be wrongly judged by anyone in your office on your taste in music. Regardless of how biased, prejudiced and unjust it may be to judge someone on their taste in music, it can and does happen. Others all too often judge people, whether it is the clothes that they wear, the cars that they drive, the towns they live in or the music that they listen to, it does happen. Music styles and certain musical artists may often have a close association with a particular belief, activity or behavior. Many artists sing about violence, sex, drugs or their own political beliefs. The act of listening to a particular type of music may be a completely acceptable behavior; however, it may not be completely appropriate in an office environment where the lyrics might offend others. Therefore, it is best to turn the music off while at the office, and simply focus on the task at hand.

Watch The Jokes

There are going to be some lighter moment occasions where you, your co-workers, your manager and possibly even your senior management will have the opportunity to talk about non-business issues, such as current events, sports, politics, etc., as well as share some personal experiences and of course the occasional joke. When participating in such discussions you must be fully aware of the content of your stories and jokes and be cautious about the impact such discussions might have on your audience.

Today's corporate America is populated with a wealth of diversity and backgrounds. Never before has our workforce seen such a broad spectrum of genders, races, religions, sexual orientations, disabilities and so on. When sharing your stories or jokes with your audience, be fully aware of the potential impact such content may have on your audience and your reputation.

It doesn't matter if you received a MBA from a top rated business school and graduated at the top of your class, if your manager, and your company perceive you as sexist, racist, or close-minded in any way, chances are that your future with your employer will be restricted in some way. Additionally, there is the potential for serious legal consequences, not just to your employer but also to you personally if it is determined that you were engaged in any form of harassment or discrimination.

The difficulty here is that in order to gain the confidence of your co-workers and manager, once in a while you will need to let your guard down and show them who you really are as a person, not just as a professional. Also, the long hours and late nights that many young professionals work can often result in a graying of the line between co-worker and friend. Young professionals have not often had sufficient experience to respect the difference between a co-worker and a true friend, and thus may find themselves in a position where they may feel comfortable sharing a certain type of joke or using certain language with a co-worker. It is here, in these circumstances, that you must be extra careful about what you are saying and how you are perceived. No matter how close you may become to your co-workers and no matter how you may perceive them more as a friend, the fact of the matter is that you are co-workers. Therefore, you must conduct yourself in a manner that respects your audience's feelings, does not represent you as derogatory or insulting, is in full compliance with current policies, laws and regulations, as well as in general accordance with overall good and decent conduct.

Young professionals should always remember that regardless of how comfortable you feel with someone in the office, regardless of how long you have worked with them, regardless of how others may act in the office, the office is the office and you should conduct yourself in a manner nothing short of entirely professional.

Young professionals must also realize that your professionalism and appropriateness of your actions are not solely restricted to the office boundaries. Whether you are playing basketball, enjoying a happy hour, playing a round of golf or any other type of social/recreational event, if you are in the presence of your co-workers, colleagues, manager or any other members associated with your employer (e.g., clients, vendors, etc.), you must conduct yourself appropriately. Just because you are not actually in the office is certainly no excuse for telling that sexually explicit joke that you just heard from a friend.

My suggestions here are to learn as much as you can about current laws concerning discrimination and harassment. Many employers require all employees to take such classes on a regular basis. However, unless you are scheduled to take such a class soon, do some homework on your own. Learn what the laws are, whom they protect, what types of actions are considered unacceptable and what the penalties are for non-compliance. At the end of the day, the best advice to offer is simply to use your best judgment and to be careful about what you say to those you have a professional relationship with. If you are the slightest bit unsure how the story or joke will be received, play it safe and keep it to yourself.

Learn The Art of Fine Dining

Whether it is a luncheon with a high profile client, a dinner event with a colleague, or a black tie affair benefiting your employer's foundation, you will likely be asked to attend some events or functions that will entail some type of fine dining. Many contacts are developed over meals and many deals are sealed over meals. Thus, you need to have an understanding of proper dining etiquette. You do not necessarily need to be a professional etiquette expert, but you should know the fundamentals of proper dining. Here are some key suggestions for your next fine dining event:

- Wait until the host of the meeting is seated before sitting down.

- Turn your cell phone off or switch it to vibrating mode. Do not answer your phone unless you know that it is a highly urgent call that cannot wait. If you must answer your phone, excuse yourself from the table before answering the call and apologize to your guests for the distraction upon your return.

- When seated, you should place your napkin on your lap. If you must leave the table, excuse yourself and place your napkin on your chair, not on the table.

- Use caution when ordering.
    - Unless you are paying for the meal, avoid high priced items on the menu.
    - Unless you are paying for the meal, follow the lead of your host when ordering appetizers and desserts.
    - Avoid messy (e.g., spaghetti) or high maintenance (e.g., whole lobster) meals.
    - Try not to order any custom made (or off the menu) dishes that may delay the time it takes to serve the other meals.
    - Do not order an alcoholic beverage unless the meal is occurring after normal work hours and then only if your host and most of the others are ordering alcoholic beverages as well. I would also strongly advise against ordering any more than one alcoholic beverage during the meal.

- Learn the layout of a formal place setting. Even some of the most seasoned dining veterans still manage to forget which is their water glass and which is their bread dish.
  - Typically, bread dishes are on your left while beverages will be on your right. A great trick is to make to "o.k." sign with both of your hands and look at the letters your fingers form. Your left hand forms the shape of the letter "b" (b = bread). Your right hand forms the shape of the letter "d" (d = drink).

- With regard to proper use of utensils, the general rule of thumb is to start from the outside working in as your proceed through the different courses of the meal.

- Wait until everyone at your table is served their meal, before beginning to eat.

- Be patient and courteous to the wait staff. Do not be demanding or degrading if your order is taking too long or if you are served the wrong dish. Never complain about the food to your dining partners or to the wait staff. You do not want to seem unappreciative.

- Generally speaking, if your order is wrong, it's best to eat what the wait staff has brought you so as not to delay the meals of others at the table. In other words, try taking one for the team!

- Do not talk with your mouth full. If you must respond while you still have food in your mouth, take your napkin and gracefully cover you mouth while you briefly respond.

- Typically you should let the host of the meal determine when it is appropriate to start talking business.

- Never ask to take home any left over food.

- Be sure to thank your host for the meal before your leave the table.

Get Involved in Your Community and Charity Causes

Corporations today are more concerned about their public image than ever before. This is the information age where news can be transmitted instantaneously and inexpensively. Substandard product quality, poor customer service, false claims, or any form of customer complaints can easily be transmitted over the internet for thousands and millions of people to see. In fact, many corporations are even monitoring online blogs about their organization or its products in the hopes of fending off negative publicity or gauging consumer interests and reactions.

Because of this greater image awareness, many companies are taking a more proactive role in developing their image as good corporate citizens. Companies are donating money to charities, donating their goods and services toward worthy causes, adopting environmental friendly policies, and asking employees to get involved in such charitable and volunteer oriented causes. This growing trend toward greater community and charity involvement must extend down to the employees who are working within the company. If it is a part of the company's mission to serve its community and those in need, it should become part of the employee's mission to serve its community and those in need. Some companies encourage employees to donate some of their company time toward a charity. Others might encourage employees to get involved in their community or join a charitable organization on their own personal time. Still other companies might not do anything to encourage their employees to get involved in such causes. Regardless of the circumstances surrounding your particular employer, you should make all reasonable efforts to donate some of your time and resources toward certain community or charity causes that are important to you and are a reflection of sound and decent principles.

Committing yourself to a community cause or charity work of some kind should first and foremost be done out of a genuine desire to help others less fortunate than you. However, you should also be aware that there are ancillary benefits to you, as a professional, by donating your time and resources to such causes. Such involvement may go a long way in supporting your image as a respectable and upright individual. As a giver to charity you are more likely to be viewed as selfless and compassionate, something that will help you develop appropriate relationships with your colleagues, co-workers, senior management and many others. As a charity giver you will be serving a personal mission that is commensurate with many corporate missions that seek to give back to their communities and assist those in need. In other words, your personal values and beliefs will be more closely aligned with the corporate values and beliefs of your employer; thus, you are more likely to be viewed as a corporate loyalist, which should improve your chances of advancing throughout the organization.

Some advice here however, is not to be overly public or outspoken about your charity work. By doing so you run the risk of appearing more self-serving than self-sacrificing. In other words, be humble about your involvement in such causes.

Be Aware of Your Purchases

Until you achieve a level of success in which your political capital, your position and your income stream substantiates a considerable level of discretionary spending, you should be aware of how your purchases may be perceived by your employer and co-workers, and how these purchases may reflect upon your character. Understand that your purchasing habits may be perceived by some as a reflection of your principles and priorities. If you are perceived as a reckless spendthrift incapable of managing your own money, how do you think your manager will perceive your ability to manage the company's money and its financial interests? Chances are not very well.

For instance, if you are not making a significant salary, are still living with your parents, have loads of college loans that you are still paying off, how do you think your manager and your company may perceive your decision to purchase that latest model BMW? Even though you may very well have inherited a considerable sum of money, and can very well afford it, management is not likely to know this; therefore, you run the risk of being perceived as somewhat careless with your finances. Try to ensure that your purchases truly and appropriately reconcile with the level of your position and the extent of your actual earnings.

If you are perceived as someone who lives beyond their means, it is possible that you will be viewed as someone who does not have sound principles and priorities. For example, if you decided to purchase a pair of high performance jet skis, but have been arriving at work late on more than a few occasions because your car has had some mechanical problems, what does this say about your priorities? This type of a decision shows a degree of financial ignorance, and suggests that your recreational activities are more important to you than your ability to get to work on time.

On the contrary, if you are a young professional who is rational with their purchases and, for the most part, acquires items of necessity with limited or appropriate extravagances, you will increase your chances of being viewed as someone who is grounded and responsible. If you are a prudent and cautious spender you will likely be viewed by management as someone who is thorough, economical and sensible. These are all essential qualities for future managers and executives.

Voice Mail Etiquette

It may sound strange but your voice mail is really an extension of you. An unprofessional sounding voice mail message will reflect poorly upon you and your professional image. Many people, who do not know you well or do not work with you on a day-to-day basis may easily form an opinion of you on such trivial things as office rumors or gossip or the way you walk, the way you dress or the way you talk, including your voice mail. When recording a message for your voice mail, be sure that your message is clear, confident, welcoming and professional. Try to avoid the dull and dreary monotone sound that most people use when leaving their voice mail message. Try leaving your message while you are in good mood and in an energized state. Leaving a message while you are frustrated or tired can affect the way you sound on your voice mail.

Try to show some excitement when leaving your message, and be sure that your tone is welcoming. That way people have a favorable opinion of you, even before they speak to you.

If your company has a standardized message that management wants employees to use, than of course use it, but again make sure that your voice is clear and audible and that the tone is welcoming and friendly. If there is not a standardized message, try a simple:

> *"Hello, you have reached __[Full Name]____ in the __[Department.]___ of __[Company]__. I apologize for not being able to answer your call; however, your call is important to me. At the end of this message, please leave your name, number and a brief message, and I will be sure to respond as soon as possible. If this is an emergency and you require immediate assistance, please press 0 and someone will help you. Have a great day and thank you for calling __[Company]__."*

Senior management or a major client who has never met you may form a poor opinion of you if they hear your voice mail say in a low, inaudible and non-welcoming tone:

> *"Hi, I'm not at my desk right now. Leave a message and I'll get back to you."*

If your job requires you to be out of the office for considerable periods of time each day, try leaving a daily tailor made message addressing your schedule for that day and indicate when you are expected to be out of the office. This will let people know when you are expected to be in the office during the day, as well as set appropriate expectations for anyone who may be expecting a prompt return call from you. For instance, you might try leaving a daily message with the following template:

> *"Hello, you have reached* __*[Full Name]*____ *in the* __*[Department]*____ *of* __*[Company]*__. *Today is* __*[Day, Date and Month]*. *I apologize for not being able to answer your call right now; however, your call is important to me. At the end of this message, please leave your name, number and a brief message, and I will be sure to respond as soon as possible. Please note that I am scheduled to be in meetings or out of the office, today from,* 9 to 10 am and 12 to 2 pm. *If this is an emergency and you require immediate assistance, please press 0 and someone will help you. Have a great day and thank you for calling* __*[Company]*__."*

If you do decide to leave a daily message on your voice mail, it is absolutely critical that you remember to change your message each day, otherwise you run the risk of appearing careless if some calls you on January 17th, and you message starts of with "Hello, Today is June 12th…."

Also, be sure to change your message when you are expected to be out of the office for any extended period of time, typically more than one business day, such as vacations, conferences, seminars, conventions, etc. Let people know when you will be back in the office and whom they can call in your absence. Most voice mail systems allow you to check your messages from off site locations. When you are not in the office, be sure to check your voice mail each day and return any important messages as soon as conveniently possible. It is also recommended that you leave a cell phone number with your boss or manager so they can reach you in the event of an emergency. A simple gesture such as leaving your personal cell phone number with your boss exhibits a strong degree of commitment and dedication to your position and its responsibilities, all of which will reflect favorably upon you.

Speakerphone Etiquette

When speaking on your phone you should be considerate of any other co-workers in close proximity to your cubicle or office. Many people are known as "speakerphone" people. These are people who strongly prefer the hands free capabilities while using the speakerphone. This allows them to do other things such as respond to emails, organize and/or file documents, or simply stand up from their desk and stare out the window while simultaneously talking on the phone. While speakerphones are an essential business tool in today's world, the fact of the matter is that they are often misused and abused by many people. The use and overuse of speakerphones can often annoy, distract and irritate other members of the office who are trying to concentrate on other tasks.

Unless you are in a private office or a remote area of the office, where few other employees are nearby, I recommend limiting the use of your speakerphone to those occasions where it is truly necessary, such as a needed group conversation where several people from one location must speak with one or more people from a separate location. In these situations, speakerphones can be very convenient and effective. Unless you have a private office and can close your door so as to prevent the disturbance of others, do not use your speakerphone so that you can clip your nails, polish your shoes, perform your office yoga routine or any other non-essential activity.

When you must use your speakerphone there are a few common courtesies that should be followed. These are as follows:

- If you are not in a strictly private location (e.g., office, conference room, etc.), and the call is scheduled ahead of time, whenever possible, try to alert employees in the immediate surrounding area of the forthcoming call so that they may adjust their schedules accordingly, if necessary. While this may not be possible every time, if you do make an effort to do this occasionally, it will send the message that you are aware of the disruption and respect the needs of others.

- Keep the speakerphone volume at a reasonable level so as not to offend others in the area.

- Regardless of whether you are initiating or receiving the call, if you are using the speakerphone, be sure to immediately alert the other party that you have them on the speakerphone. Sometimes your caller may think things are being said in the strictest of confidence when in fact, if they are on the speakerphone, many others in the area may hear them. For instance,

> *"Good morning John, it's great to talk to you again. Just so that you are aware, I have you on speakerphone right now."*

- Speak up. Speakerphone technology has come a long way over the years, but it is still evolving and can still be a source of confusion and frustration. Unless you are seated in very close proximity to the speakerphone, it may be difficult for your listeners to hear you, so be sure to speak loud enough so that they can hear you. This is amongst the many reasons why over using the speakerphone can be very distracting to others in your area. During your first contact with the caller, inquire whether they can hear you and adjust your speaking volume as needed.

> *"John, this is Dave Winston speaking right now, I'm the regional manager for your area. Just so that you are aware, I have you on speakerphone right now. Can you hear me O.K.?"*

- After informing the other party that you have them on speakerphone and inquiring if they can hear you, advise them exactly who is the room with you listening to or participating in the call.

> *"Good morning John, it's great to talk to you again. Just so that you are aware, I have you on speakerphone right now. In the room, I have with me, Tom Jennings, your new account representative and Dave Winston our regional manager. Shall we begin?"*

- Introduce yourself when entering into the conversation. Because of the multiple parties on the line, this will inform the listeners exactly who is speaking at the moment.

> *"John, this is Dave Winston, I'm the regional manager for your area, and I just wanted to tell you how happy we are to have your business..."*

> *"John, this is Tom Jennings, I've been assigned to your account. I am so pleased to be working with you and your organization..."*

Sit Straight

As young children, many of us were scolded by our parents or our teachers for slouching in our chairs and not sitting straight. I recall thinking to myself, what difference does it make whether I slouch or sit straight up in my chair, I am still sitting, I am still listening, so who really cares? However, most of us seem to agree that the appearance of a young man or woman, casually slouching in their chair in a formal workplace setting (e.g., meeting) appears to exhibit a degree of carelessness, disrespect for the speaker and possibly even laziness. Thus, it would seem practical that young professionals should act in a manner that helps them to be perceived in a manner that is appropriate and professional.

Whenever you are at a sit down meeting, luncheon or any other type of face-to-face gathering, it is important that young professionals show other individuals at the meeting respect and good manners by sitting straight in their chairs with full attention being given to the person speaking. Doing so will illustrate the young professional as someone who is attentive, respectful, polite and interested in what the speaker has to say.

Be Brief

Keep your communications brief and to the point. By communications, I am referring to memorandums, emails, letters, reports, as well as verbal presentations, remarks or statements. Young professionals must understand that managers, and senior management often have insanely hectic schedules and don't have the time to read or listen to a lengthy description of every one of their employee's questions, concerns or comments.

Young professionals should match the length and depth of their communications to the severity of the issue. Your manager simply doesn't have the luxury of reading a 5-page memorandum on how you think color-coding the filing system might help improve efficiency. However, if the issue concerns a operational weakness that jeopardizes the company's products or services, adversely affects corporate profitability or could potentially place the company in a precarious legal position I am sure that your manager would gladly review a comprehensive assessment of the topic. Young professionals who do not understand this concept can often "write themselves out" of an issue, because in many cases a manager is not likely to read, or fully read, a multi-page memorandum on a non-essential or trivial topic such as how you think the company could save $12 each month by switching coffee vendors. Even on more important issues, if the correspondence is too long, too confusing, or poorly written, your manager is much more likely to put that piece of correspondence down and attend to other matters first. If this happens, the odds of your manager ever picking up that report ever again are remote at best. If you manager or a senior manager is trying to burn through a 2 foot thick stack of stuff in his or her in-box before their next meeting which begins in 15 minutes, your 5 page memo will not likely stand a chance of being read, unless the issue is critical and essential.

When preparing your communications, follow these rules:

- Match the length and depth of detail in your communication to the severity and importance of the topic.

- Summarize the purpose of your communication upfront, and describe how this issue is important to your manager, the group or the company. The following language is an example of what I am referring to here:

> "The purpose of this correspondence is to bring to your attention a problem with how the monthly divisional sales reports are prepared. For the reasons stated herein, these reports may be inaccurate and misleading. Given that senior management relies upon this information to make certain strategic decisions, I am compelled to provide you with this correspondence…"

- Use footnotes, addendums, schedules or attachments to capture appropriate data or information that may be relevant to the issue, but not important enough to include in the body of your primary correspondence.

- Stick to the point, do not get sidetracked with unnecessary details, data or information. If necessary, further communications can be used to further support your idea, issue or thought.

- When presenting a verbal comment, thought or question to someone, before you blurt out your idea, show some respect by asking that person if they have a moment of time to spare for you, and also attempt to quantify how much time you may need from them. For instance,

> "Excuse me Mr. Manager, do you have time for a quick question, it should only take a minute or two of your time."

This allows that person to consider his or her present schedule and tasks to determine if he or she has sufficient time at the moment or whether they will need you to come back at a later time.

Play The Name Game

I can recall a seminar that I once took on strengthening interpersonal skills. As the students were arriving for the class, the instructor stood in the doorway of the classroom and introduced himself to each of the 75 or so students. With each student who entered the classroom he thanked him or her for attending the class and politely inquired what their name was. No one was wearing nametags and never once did I notice him write anything down on paper. Once everyone was seated, he started the class by going around the classroom and repeated everyone's name from memory. He did it quickly and did not get one name wrong! Everyone was impressed and curious how he did that.

A person's name is amongst their most personal and special possessions. A person's name is private, exclusive and a shinning symbol of that person's value and beliefs. A person's name is their identity. A person's name is quite simply, who they are. When someone remembers your name, particularly if it is someone that you are not very familiar with, most people are favorably influenced. When someone remembers your name, it can make some of us feel special and significant. Anyone who has been graciously greeted at the front door of their favorite restaurant with a "Good evening Mr. Smith, it is nice to see you again. How are you tonight?" knows what I am talking about. Remembering someone's name is a simple gesture that reaches the inner most depths of a person's being and warms their core. Remembering someone's name is a significant technique that can be used to build rapport and develop both personal and professional relationships.

Equally important is the social disruption and embarrassment that often follows when you find yourself in a situation where you realize that you should remember someone's name, but can't. If you have met someone before, have spoken with them before, but cannot remember their name, how do you think that makes them feel? Chances are, not very good. Not recalling someone's name can signal to them that you don't think that they are important enough to remember them, that you weren't really paying attention to them when you were first introduced or that you simply don't care about developing a relationship with them. In any of these cases, you are going to have some obstacles to overcome in developing a meaningful connection with that person. Yes, you can always ask their name again, but by doing so, you are effectively eliminating the intrinsic value and significance that is gained by remembering that person's name in the first place. So the best advice on this topic is to get it right the first time. A fine tuned skill of remembering names is a potent weapon in your arsenal of tools that can be used to develop meaningful relationships with co-workers, colleagues, management, senior executives and clients.

There are a many memory-enhancing techniques that can be utilized to assist you in remembering names. Many books and articles have been written solely on this topic; however, here are a few key pointers:

- *Make a commitment.* When you are meeting someone, pledge to yourself to make a commitment to learn his or her name. Focus on them, and only them. Truly listen as they introduce themselves. Don't get distracted.

- *If necessary, during the initial encounter, ask them to repeat their name.* If you did not hear them the first time, politely ask them to repeat their name again. Do not let this opportunity pass; there are no second chances.

- *Use the name (but don't overuse it).* It is important that you use the person's name during your initial encounter with them, but equally important is not to over use it. Using the person's name a few times during a five to ten minute conversation is acceptable. Also, when closing the encounter be sure to state the person's name as you are leaving. For instance, "John, it has been a real pleasure speaking with you tonight, enjoy the rest of the evening." Using the person's name will also help solidify it in your memory.

- *Spell the name in your mind three times.* At the conclusion of your introduction spell the person's name in your mind three times. This will help "burn" the image in your mind so that it is easier to recall in the future.

- *Association.* Associate the person's name with something that you are familiar with. For instance, if you meet someone named William, and enjoy reading Shakespeare, associate this new person with William Shakespeare.

- *Get a Business Card.* While on business, if you are speaking with someone whom you have something in common with or if there is a potential business relationship (e.g., work for the same company, work in the same industry, prospective client, etc.), ask for his or her business card. After the encounter put the business card in your contact database with some personal notes about the person. For instance, you might write down how many children they have, a favorite hobby or interest or their favorite sports team. If you meet again, not only will you remember their name, but you might also remember something personal about them, which will further help you to build a stronger rapport with them.

Dress Code vs. Fashion Code

If you are working in a professional office, where the standard dress code is a traditionally formal environment (e.g., suits, jackets, ties, etc.), follow the lead of the company's senior management in terms of your own personal dress code, even though your manager or co-workers may be allowed to dress more casually. Doing so indicates that you take your position seriously, that you respect the responsibilities of your position and that you wish to be viewed as a professional.

Also, while most companies may have a dress code, few if any, have a true "fashion" code. For instance, a company's dress code might indicate that males are expected to wear neatly pressed suits, collared shirts, ties and dress shoes. However, this description truly fails to outline what types of suits, shirts, ties and shoes are really acceptable and appropriate. For instance, assume that you are working in a large investment bank where most senior and executive managers are known to wear single-breasted gray or blue suits, a starched white shirt, conventional and conservative patterned ties with black wing tip shoes. Now picture yourself coming to work in an olive green double-breasted suit, a pink shirt, a tie with a digitally enhanced picture of your dog on it and burgundy loafers. While your attire is likely in compliance with the organization's dress code, it is clearly outside the boundaries of the organization's unwritten "fashion" code. Thus, be sure that you are not only informed about the formal dress code of your organization, but also be aware of the specific types, styles and colors of clothing that is considered acceptable and appropriate. In order to gauge the nature of your company's fashion code, it is best to consider the types and styles of clothing being worn by high ranking, long standing or senior executive members of the organization. This is not to say that you need to wear the same top designer name brands as those that might be worn by senior management. Rather, simply consider the colors, styles and types of clothing that is worn by senior management and adopt a wardrobe that is consistent with that of senior management.

In addition, take notice of any accompanying accoutrements or accessories that may routinely accompany the office wear of senior management. For instance, if a considerable portion of senior management does not wear suspenders, I would suggest that you avoid them as well. Does senior management all wear lapel pins with the company's logo on it? If so, try finding out how to acquire one, and wear it on your suit lapel each day.

With regards to your suit jacket, while you may not necessarily need to wear your suit jacket at your desk or in your respective department, be sure to always have your suit jacket available. In other words, do not leave it at home or in your car. If you are ever asked to go to the executive suite area of the building, or any other areas where senior or executive management may be, be sure to put your suit jacket on. This seemingly insignificant task sends the right message to management that you respect their authority, their positions and are seeking their approval about being viewed as a professional.

Also, whenever visiting a public area of the organization such as a bank branch, retail showroom, sales floor or any other place where you are likely to be seen by clients or the public, wear your suit jacket. Again, this shows respect for your company's clients and indicates that you take your responsibility as a representative of your company seriously and professionally.

Don't Overdo It

Many of us can spot a fake laugh a mile away. Consistently laughing at a bad joke, just because your boss told it is simply not necessary to advance yourself in your career. In fact, you may be doing more harm than good as many of us can clearly see that those laughing with feign and insincerity are clearly kissing up to the boss. Clearly, you must treat your boss with the respect that he or she deserves as your superior; however, you do not need to compliment your boss on his tie everyday, offer to get him a fresh cup of coffee, run personal errands for them or laugh falsely at their jokes.

Doing something genuine, out of the goodness of your heart, is vastly different than doing something just to score points with the boss. If you develop a reputation as someone who kisses up to the boss, the risks are twofold. First, you run the risk of being exiled by your peers and colleagues. Respect from your peers is not earned by way of kissing up to the boss; it is earned through hard work and determination. Without this respect you may find it increasingly difficult to complete tasks and assignments where the assistance of your peers and colleagues may be crucially necessary. Second, you may lose respect from your boss. Many individuals who have supervisory and managerial experience can often spot someone who is deceitful and false-hearted with relative ease. While management styles and personalities do differ greatly, the rules of corporate America unmistakably fail to endorse or sanction disingenuous acts of kindness just to gain favor with the boss.

While it is true that some managers may greatly enjoy the ego boosting affects of such behavior, it is just not worth the risk to the young professional. It is not worth risking the adverse impact that this behavior could have to one's reputation and political capital. It is not worth risking potential damage to any critical relationships within the organization to engage in such falsehoods. Once again, while young professionals must be sure to treat their superiors with the respect that they deserve as senior members of the organization, young professionals must however, adopt a firm belief that the only way to gain favor with such senior members is through a strong work ethic, professional expertise, technical skills and talents and developing an impressive record of accomplishments. There are simply no shortcuts.

Take Lunch...With Others

While many of us may anxiously await and greatly enjoy the downtime, relaxation and humor from a select few of our close co-workers during lunch, you should make a concerted effort to eat lunch with other employees in the company. Regularly dining with other employees of the company will offer the following benefits to you:

- Expand your contacts and enhance your networking capacities within the company,

- Successfully illustrate your ability to easily step outside your "comfort zone" and a capability of conversing and socializing with a variety of different people, which is an important characteristic of many senior level executives,

- Provide you with insight into other areas of the company, which will educate you on the purpose, operations, and personnel of other departments within the organization.

I would not recommend that you randomly select individuals in the company to ask out to lunch. Do some homework and find out who everybody is, what they do, what their backgrounds are, etc. Then after you have gathered some of this information, select some key people who may have impressive backgrounds, experiences that you admire or positions that you are interested in, and introduce yourself to them. For instance, if you are currently occupying a back office position in a large investment bank, and are interested in getting into a more exciting area of the organization, such as mergers and acquisitions, try finding someone who works in that area and ask them to have lunch with you so you can pick their brain a bit. You do not necessarily need to find a senior level managing director of M&A. Rather you could try finding someone who is more your peer that happens to work in that particular area of the company. Introduce yourself, indicate what department you work in, how long you have been with the company and indicate that you are interested in learning more about their area. Then politely ask them if they would be kind enough to have lunch with you one day. As an enticement, offer to buy them lunch at their favorite restaurant. Indicate that you are interested in learning more about the area that they work in, such as what the requirements are to obtain a position in that department, what the challenges are, what the incentives are and so forth.

Even if someone declines or asks you for a rain check, you have most likely been successful at making a positive impression on that person simply by introducing yourself and taking the initiative to learn more about something that interests you. If they accept, be sure to prepare some intelligent questions and talking points ahead of time. Who knows, the person you are eating with might be your future supervisor, so treat the lunch as a formal meeting.

I am not saying that you need to, nor should you, go out for lunch every day with a different person. In fact, I am a firm believer in working lunches most of the times. Working lunches say a lot about a person's work ethic and character. However, everyone needs a change of scenery or a breath of fresh air occasionally. My point here is that when you do decide to go out for lunch, you should not go out with the same few people every time. Rather use some strategic judgment and ask someone whom you might find interesting or intellectually rewarding to have lunch with you. If you are successful at implementing this strategy for an extended period of time, you will be surprised at the extent and breadth of contacts that you will have developed. You will also be surprised at how much you have learned about different areas of the organization.

Keep An Open Door Policy

While many young professionals may not necessarily be accommodated with their own private office in the early part of their career, it is still important that you keep a so-called "open door policy". In other words, you should make yourself available to assist others whenever reasonably possible so as to further support your reputation as a team player and someone willing to work toward the greater good of the group, division and ultimately the entire organization. Making yourself available to answer questions, proof work, test reasoning or simply provide assistance or guidance will assist you in developing a positive and favorable reputation within the group which will enhance your political capital throughout the organization.

If for some reason you are approached for some guidance and are in the midst of an important and time sensitive project or task, politely explain your current situation to the other person and ask them if you can assist them once you finish what you are doing. To help them understand when they might expect your assistance, set an estimated timeframe as to when you might expect to have more time to devote to them. Is it in a couple minutes, a couple hours, tomorrow or is it next week? If you get the sense that they need some assistance immediately, and you cannot provide it to them, offer them a reasonable alternative such as directing them to someone else who might be capable of helping them or pointing them in the direction of a resource where they may find their answers (e.g., policies, procedures, etc.). That way, even when you do not have the time to meet or talk with them, you are still assisting them by providing them with some useful information that might benefit them.

Maintaining a favorable reputation within your group is important since it will serve to promote you well throughout the entire organization. Maintaining a favorable reputation with your co-workers and peers is also important since you never know when you may need their assistance. If you take some extra time out of your day to help one of your co-workers, they are much more likely to assist you in the same way when you are in need of similar help.

Learn To Take Criticism

As a young professional you need to be able to handle criticism. While you may have achieved a nearly perfect score on your SAT's and you may have had a perfect 4.0 GPA in college; the corporate world is much different than academia. In fact, as a new employee you are essentially starting from scratch. You will need to learn through training; you will need to learn through hard work; you will need to learn through self-discipline and sacrifice and yes, you will need to learn from your mistakes. As such, with these mistakes, you must be able to handle some criticism from your manager.

Handling criticism is difficult for most of us, regardless of our age or experience. However, young professionals have not had a lot of experience in the corporate world. Young professionals are generally accustomed to the sensitive and softened critiques of college professors such as "Good answer, but not quite what I'm looking for" rather than the hard-core corporate response of "What the hell were you thinking? Do you have any idea how much money this mistake could have cost us?" Statements like that are easy to dampen anyone's confidence. More importantly, if you are unable to successfully handle criticism, it is easy to get demoralized and unmotivated, which can clearly taint one's confidence and ultimately destroy one's performance.

The keys to effectively handling criticism at work are as follows:

- *Don't take it personally.* Criticism at work does not generally involve personal attacks on one's character; so do not misinterpret the message.

- *Stay calm and don't argue back.* Arguing with your manager or supervisor will typically only make things worse and escalate the issue beyond its true value. If you firmly believe that the criticism is misdirected or inappropriate for some reason, state you case, but do so delicately and respectfully, but do not yell or scream, do not interrupt your manager or supervisor and never make excuses for your mistake.

- *Consider who is delivering the criticism.* If you are being berated by your direct supervisor who has little authority or political capital and carries little weight in shaping your career, don't get too upset about it. Listen to them, but don't lose any sleep over it. However, if you are being criticized by someone you greatly respect and admire, someone who has great authority within the organization and someone who holds great political capital, try speaking to him or her about your situation. If it was an honest mistake on your part, own up to it.

- *Consider the ultimate source of the criticism.* In addition to who is delivering the criticism, consider who or how the criticism came to fruition. For instance, criticism that perhaps originated from a disgruntled co-worker who you recently surpassed for a recent promotion is much less significant than criticism originating from a high-ranking member of the organization or a highly valued client.

- *Prioritize the criticism appropriately.* Each of the many tasks that you do each day, and each of the responsibilities you have, have a level of priority associated with them. Don't worry about criticism associated with low priority tasks or insignificant responsibilities. For instance, if you were traveling all last week and successfully landed the largest sale of the year, and are now being criticized for not completing your expense voucher correctly, don't loose sleep over it. Keep the big picture in mind.

<u>Find A Stress Outlet</u>

Regardless of how well you are capable of handling criticism, regardless of how effective you are at keeping your emotions in check and regardless of how well you perform under pressure, the incessant demands of your work will undoubtedly have an adverse affect on your attitude and your performance if not carefully and properly managed. The ability to handle stress is much like the elasticity of a balloon as it is being inflated. It allows someone to adapt to the changing demands of their environment (e.g., increasing levels of stress). However, much like every balloon, every person has a point of no return, where the demands are so great that we will eventually "pop", unless that stress is truly released. As a young professional "pops" under the pressure, they may fall into a temper tantrum of some form, they may break down in tears, they may storm out of the office in anger or they may start saying things that they don't truly mean or are not reflective of their true character, none of which would be good for one's career.

Thus, young professionals must be successful at finding effective stress outlets. Stress outlets are a key component of all comprehensive stress management programs and critical to one's long-term survival in the corporate world. Stress outlets should be employed on a regular basis by the young professional, not solely on an as needed basis. Much like that balloon in the aforementioned example, many young professionals are not fully in tune with how successful or unsuccessful they are at handling stress. As some of you may have noticed, there are many cases where someone seems to be in a fine mood, but then without warning or notice, suddenly "pops." Utilizing an effective stress outlet on a regular basis will ensure that the project you are presently working on, the person that you are speaking with or the boss that you are listening to is never that catalyst that causes you to "pop."

I would advise you to speak with your physician about effective stress outlets for you based upon your age, health conditions, occupation, etc. However, many common stress outlets include the following:

- Regular exercise,

- Hobbies (e.g., photography, painting, music, cooking, etc.),

- Relaxation techniques, (e.g., yoga),

Enhance Group Synergy

All too often departments, groups, or teams of employees that work together will fail to truly identify with each other as individuals. Many may know the names and faces of those they work with; however, many simply fail to understand exactly who their co-workers and colleagues really are, what they stand for and what their beliefs and values are. Many times, we might be closely familiar with our co-workers and colleagues as employees and corporate citizens, but not as real individuals.

You do not need to understand the specific personal details of each and every co-worker or colleague that you have some encounter with; however, it is important that you develop a relationship that is supportive, productive, respectful and valuable. The closer you understand each other, the better you will be able to understand what motivates each other, what interests each other, what upsets each other, etc. With this knowledge, one can manage personal encounters within the group or department so as to achieve optimum performance. Obtaining this knowledge can often be difficult, particularly if one attempts to do it solely at the office and on corporate time. Additionally, corporate time should be spent on corporate issues, tasks and problems. Nonetheless, you can make some reasonable efforts to get to know each of your co-workers and colleagues, as real individuals, through alternative means. Doing so should ultimately facilitate stronger group dynamics including better communication, higher productivity, greater synergy, etc. Some possible techniques might include the following:

- Arranging a monthly or quarterly luncheon or dinner with all group members,

- Hosting an annual group barbeque or picnic at your home or in a nearby park,

- Coordinating a regular sporting event for all group members to participate in, such as softball, basketball, etc.,

- Organizing a regular card game with all of your appropriate co-workers and colleagues.

A critical piece of advice to consider is when you are coordinating such an event to be sure not to exclude anyone in your group or office. Do not be selective in who you choose to invite. Make it an open invite to all those in your department or group. That way you cannot be accused of excluding anyone, which could serve to damage your reputation and create unnecessary tension within the group.

Given that such events will typically be held off hours and outside the office, it may be acceptable to turn up the music, have some fun, play some games, tell some appropriate jokes, but do not forget that while you may be out of the office, you are still amongst your office contemporaries. Therefore, while you may feel somewhat more relaxed than if you were in the office, many of the rules of conduct and appropriate behavior discussed herein will still apply. Stay away from politically charged topics (e.g., religion, politics, etc.), do not drink excessive amounts of alcohol, etc. Just because you are out of the office, dressed casually and sharing a robust round of laughter, you are not relieved of your responsibilities of acting with decorum, respect and decency at such events. Keep this in mind.

Ideas such as those listed above signal that you are serious about developing a meaningful and productive relationship with those that you work with. Not only will you be given credit for strengthening the group dynamics, increasing efficiencies, enhancing productivity, reducing group tensions, etc., you will be given some leadership kudos for taking the initiative and coordinating the event(s). Any efforts that you can make to increase the effectiveness and efficiencies within your group will serve you and your reputation extremely well.

Create Value for Yourself

A great way to stand out from your competition (e.g., coworkers) is to develop a skill or an ability that is needed in your department and that no one else knows or possesses. This will help you stand out from the crowd and will also help increase your value to the department, and thus, the company. I'm not talking about knowing how to change the toner cartridge or free the photocopier of a paper jam, I'm talking about material tasks or jobs that in some way make your manager's job easier, faster or better. I'm talking about jobs or tasks that add value to the operations of your department. Be creative when searching for these unique ways to create value for yourself. It may be something like writing formulas or macro commands within a spreadsheet application. It may be something like knowing how to perform a merge letter function from a database application so as to facilitate a mass mailing to all of the company's clients. It may be something like knowing how to manipulate a certain report writing software application so as to improve the group's information management capabilities.

A good place to start is by reviewing the day-to-day operations of your department. Review a departmental workflow diagram and review specific operating procedures and ask yourself "How can I make this function easier or faster?" Ask yourself, "How can I automate this function?" Ask yourself, "How can I get more timely or more accurate information to those who need it?" Review the departmental operations relative to these questions and starting thinking of a way that you can enhance the effectiveness or efficiency of certain tasks. Once you have identified an appropriate area that you wish to focus on, start reviewing the possible solutions to achieving your goal. Consider all of the technological capacities that you have at your disposal by way of your existing network and other software applications and determine whether there are any overlooked or underutilized features that may assist you. Consider speaking to a trusted colleague in the Information and Technologies Department for technological assistance.

After some time, it is possible, even likely, that other employees will learn how you perform these specific tasks or duties. This will either be achieved through a directive issued by your manager to instruct them how the task works, or it may happen over time through operational absorption. Whatever the case, once others learn how your new and improved idea works, your value to the group will have been reduced since there will be others on staff that can do the same thing. Therefore,

93

you should constantly be searching for ways to improve existing processes, overcome obstacles or solve relevant problems. Never stop searching for ways to improve your value to your manager, the group and ultimately the organization.

Smile

There is an overlooked tool that many young professionals often fail to use in developing their career. This tool has the ability to aid you in developing strategic alliances within the group, the company and the entire industry. This tool will help you build important mentoring relationships. This tool will help you develop critical relationships that may be essential to your professional development, productivity and political capital. This tool will help you create an overall positive image for yourself. This tool will help draw people toward you, from which you can strengthen your interpersonal and social skills. This tool is a simple and sincere "smile" from time to time.

A smile is a signal to those around you that you are approachable and accessible. A smile is a reflection of your mood and your personality. A genuine smile is welcoming and comforting. People simply do not enjoy being around miserable and unhappy people, and in some cases will avoid them at all costs. Thus, if you are constantly walking around the office with a perma-smug on your face, you are severely limiting your ability to develop critical relationships with key individuals who might be able to assist you in developing your skills and advancing your career. Whether you are in need of a true mentor, a technical guru or simply a trusted and loyal colleague, you are much more likely to develop these critical relationships throughout your career if you posture yourself as a warm and welcoming individual, someone that others enjoy being around. This all begins with a simple smile.

Understand the Rules of Personal Conversations and Office Gossip

Refrain from engaging in office gossip and extended chatter with your co-workers. Clearly, you need to develop a rapport with your co-workers and colleagues so you can establish a line into the company grapevine and develop appropriate relationships and alliances. However, you need to know the rules of personal conversations and office gossip. Be sure that you are disciplined in the amount of time you spend talking with them about non-business issues. Be sure that it is done during appropriate times and that you respect the other employees in the area who may be trying to work. Also, when you do decide to engage in such gossip or chatter, be cautious about what information you are sharing with your co-workers.

Be cognizant about "lingering" in the hallways or around a co-workers desk for too long. Extended chatter with your co-workers is not going to assist you in persuading your manager and senior management that you have a strong and disciplined work ethic. Doing so also appears that you have nothing better or more important to do. This is probably not the message that you are trying to send to your manager.

While everyone needs to "step away" from what they are doing once in a while, be sure that you limit the amount of personal conversations that you have in the office, be sure that such conversations are held only during appropriate times and be sure that such conversations are not adversely directed at other co-workers, clients or company policies. For instance, if you have just been assigned a critical project and are working under a strict deadline, now is probably not the time to engage in any form of non-business conversation. Imagine if your boss just assigned you a critical task 30 minutes ago, and asked you to complete it as soon as possible, then she sees you standing next to one of your co-workers discussing the fashion choices of one of your co-workers or any other immaterial, non-pertinent, non-business issue.

Also, be aware of how loud you and your co-workers are speaking. At the end of a long and productive workweek, when you have completed all of your assignments, you might find yourself in a carefree personal conversation with your co-workers. However, while you and your co-workers may agree that you deserve a little "down time" you must respect the other employees around you and understand that they might still be attempting to finish their work. In many cases, other employees may be on the phone with a client, a senior manager or any other high level employee. I do not imagine that the client, senior manger or director on the other end of the phone will enjoy hearing a robust round of laughter in the background of their conversation with that employee.

When you do decide to engage in an occasional personal conversation during office time, try to stick to non-personal, inoffensive and innocuous issues such as the economy, sports, recent news stories, etc. In other words, do not revisit your weekend's foray with your co-workers at the office. If you do, you run the risk of your boss hearing, or others gossiping, about that drunken bar crawl that you were on Saturday night. Stay away from any issue, topic or story that doesn't portray you in a favorable manner.

Also, never engage yourself in a conversation where your co-workers are speaking poorly about your boss, senior management, your company, its policies, a client, etc. Such criticism is negative, immature and can serve you no good. If you are over heard, or are simply guilty by association in such a situation, you could be viewed as unkind and callous, which could do great damage to your efforts to develop additional political capital, especially if you have to explain yourself. If you are involved in a conversation that does turn to such personal criticisms, just walk away as if you have an important assignment that needs to be completed.

In sum, here are the ground rules of office gossip and personal chatter:

- Keep it brief, and do not linger. Get into the conversation and get out.

- If you do decide to engage in some personal conversations with your co-workers, be sure that it is an appropriate time.

- Watch the volume, and respect the work of others around you.

- Stick to issues that are innocent and harmless, that will not reflect poorly upon you.

- Never speak poorly about others. If others do, leave the conversation immediately.

Stay Late

It is critical, especially during the early part of your career, that you not be viewed as the proverbial "nine to five'er." Be prepared to sacrifice yourself and some of your personal time to the organization. If you are expecting to be treated as a professional, you must act like a professional and be prepared to make some personal sacrifices. That means staying late, and putting in the time, when something needs to get done.

Like it or not, those whose show up at 8:59 am and leave at 5:01 pm are typically perceived as individuals willing to give only the bare minimum to their employers. Try to recognize the true value of your position within the context of the group and the entire organization, and try to understand that your responsibilities may not necessarily end at 5:00 pm each day. Some may say "Well, everyone else is leaving at 5:00 pm, so why shouldn't I?" If you work in such an environment, this is a unique and somewhat easy opportunity for you to truly distance yourself from your competing co-workers and colleagues, and a great opportunity to build a strong reputation as a hard and diligent worker simply by putting in a little extra time each day.

Many managers may fully expect their employees to stay later, come in earlier, or on an occasional weekend, or simply give a little extra effort. However, many managers may not necessarily communicate these expectations to their employees, either because they are too timid or too fearful of damaging employee morale. Some might simply believe that their employees should be putting in such extra efforts without having to be instructed to do so. Regardless, the expectation of extra efforts, above and beyond what is typically required is there, and it is real.

It is also advised that you find an occasional weekend to visit the office, even if just for a few moments to "clean up some loose ends." This will give you some insight into what the work ethic is for your office during weekends. If there is no one else there, just take an hour or two to catch up on some work that you left behind on Friday or to get ahead for Monday. If the office is filled with your co-workers and colleagues, than you may have to do the same in order to compete effectively for future opportunities in the group. Without the distractions of constant visitors, phone calls, and emails, those precious few hours of work on a Saturday or Sunday can often be the equivalent of full day's productivity during a weekday. While no one may necessarily enjoy the idea of coming into the office on a weekend, as a young professional, this is a great way to greatly enhance your productivity in a short amount of time and build a positive and favorable reputation for yourself.

In the end, consider the first few years with your employer to be your corporate "boot camp." Be prepared to work harder, faster and longer than you ever have before. Also, consider that the extra efforts you exert in the early part of your career will serve you well in developing a strong and favorable reputation throughout the organization. Once you have achieved this, and have successfully made some advancement, you may likely find yourself in a position where you can scale back such efforts since you will have climbed a little higher on the learning curve. In summary, some rules of thumb to consider here include:

- Stay later than the great majority of your co-workers,

- Never leave before your boss,

- Visit your office on an occasional weekend,

- Acknowledge that your first few years of employment will be your corporate "boot camp".

Attend Corporate Functions

As a professional, you will be expected to perform your day-to-day responsibilities and meet established expectations in the office. However, you will also be expected to present yourself in a public and social setting in a manner fitting of a true professional. Management will expect you to be capable of carrying on extemporaneous conversations with individuals whom you may never have met before. Management will expect you to attend such events as the company holiday party, summer picnic, corporate retreat or simply the occasional boss sponsored happy hour after a job well done. The underlying purposes of such events are not necessarily entirely social. These events provide management with a small glimpse into how their employees conduct themselves in a relaxed and social atmosphere. A certain employee may be an outstanding young marketing professional who has displayed an extraordinary level of creativity in the office. However, he or she may not have the social skills to present and sell their ideas to clients. These events often allow management to assess employees' interpersonal skills and other such characteristics.

Not only do these events offer management an opportunity to assess an employee's interpersonal and social skills, but attending such events also shows management that you are capable of waving the company flag and displaying your corporate spirit. Attending these events shows management that you are, in many ways, a dedicated and faithful employee who is willing to sacrifice some of their own personal time for the benefit of the organization, and its mission.

A word of caution here however; if you are able to invite a guest to a corporate event, unless you are married or engaged, it is best if you attend the event alone. While you may have been dating the same person for some time, there is no guarantee that you will be dating them at next year's holiday party. You do not want to be seen at various corporate events with slew of different people. This shows a degree of instability and possibly a level of immaturity, not an ideal characteristic of an up a coming young professional.

Find Your Shepherds

In an earlier tip we discussed the importance of understanding what political capital is, and how it works. Once a young professional understands political capital they can begin preparation for truly leveraging it to their advantage.

Clearly talent directly influences one's ability to advance throughout an organization; however, young professionals can further support their ability to advance by way of reputable sponsorship from someone with great political capital. In corporate America, employees are often promoted for one of two reasons. Either because the employee has proven their ability or because someone of great importance in the organization is willing to endorse the employee's ability and recommend them for a promotion. In some cases, this person might be the person that the young professional directly reports to, but it does not necessarily have to be. In some cases, a young professional's direct manager or supervisor might be too lazy, too busy or simply may not truly believe in the young professional's ability, all of which could delay or stall the young professional's advancement. Because of this, it is not practical to rely solely upon the one person that you report to for advancing your career.

Therefore, young professionals should seek to identify a few key individuals within the organization and strive hard to impress these individuals. These individuals should be people who have strong political capital within the organization and have the power and authority to influence careers.

Because these people have the means to take someone from one place to another, and will often look out for the best interests of others, I refer to these key individuals as corporate "shepherds." Your shepherd may or may not be the person you directly report to. Your shepherd might be someone whom you might not have any direct day-to-day contact with. Nonetheless, your shepherd should be someone who has the power to promote your strongest qualities amongst their colleagues and throughout the organization and thus advance your career. Here are some tips on how to select the right shepherd:

- It is essential that your shepherd have a strong political capital base. Often (but not always) this equates to a member of senior management, one who has been with the company a considerable period of time, one with a proven record of accomplishment and one who is accepted and respected amongst members of senior and executive management.

- Do not overachieve in selecting your shepherd. In other words, it might not be practical to select the CEO as your shepherd; however, it may be a key middle manager that is closely aligned, and in good favor, with the CEO. In other words, the hectic schedules of most executives and the subsequent lack of time that they typically have to get to know each staff member may make it difficult for a top level executive to act as your shepherd. However, you can often accomplish the same objective by identifying key individuals who typically have the confidence of, and routinely "have the ear" of those top-level executives. If you are successful at influencing these individuals, they will likely report back to the top-level executives about your strong potential and good prospects, which in the end will accomplish much the same as if you had directly influenced that top level executive directly.

- Be cautious about being perceived as someone who is "kissing up" when designing strategies to impress and win the respect of your shepherd. In other words, do not offer to wash your shepherd's car, or pick up her dry cleaning. Keep your strategies professional and strictly business related. For instance, if you happen to know that your shepherd is preparing a PowerPoint presentation for an upcoming board meeting, you might inform them that you recently just took a PowerPoint class and would be glad to utilize some of your new skills in helping her assemble the presentation.

- Select no less than three, but no more than five shepherds. If you were to view the selection of a shepherd as a bet, you should try to hedge your bet by selecting several key individuals to act as your shepherds. This also helps to mitigate the risk of wasted efforts in the event your one shepherd were to leave the company or suffer a setback to his or her political capital. Equally important, however, is not to select too many shepherds otherwise your return might not be as significant. If you seek to gain the respect of too many individuals, you might be spreading yourself too thin to make any significant impact on these individuals. It's best to be somewhat selective in terms of who you are attempting to impress, and then let them and their networking throughout the organization spread the good word about your abilities and potential.

Before leaving this tip, I want to make sure that we are clear on one thing. Your efforts to select, impress and gain the respect of your shepherds must be above and beyond your efforts and abilities to perform the day-to-day responsibilities of your current position. Your efforts to impress your shepherds will be meaningless and insignificant if they are later informed that you are not meeting the basic requirements of your current position within the company. If you just started with your employer or recently assumed a new position, try focusing the first six to nine months solely on your current position and all of its corresponding responsibilities. After you have gained some confidence in your position and received some positive feedback about your performance, that is when you can start the process of identifying a shepherd or two, and making a positive impression on them.

Find Your Mentors

As it is often said, "knowledge is power." Regardless of the industry you are in or the position you hold, when seeking to advance yourself through the organization, having a broader and deeper knowledge base than others is amongst the most potent weapons a young professional may possess. Knowing more than the person sitting next to you places you at a tremendous advantage when it is time for allocating bonuses or filling a senior position in the group. Unfortunately, for whatever the reasons, whether it may be the increasing costs, inadequate return on investment or outright lack of commitment on behalf of management, many companies appear to have abandoned the various formal training programs geared toward developing young talent. Many of these programs were often an extension of undergraduate and graduate level studies with a combination of extensive classroom based learning, case study scenarios and real life challenges and responsibilities. An employee who has been chosen to participate in such a training program is given a prestigious opportunity within the organization to increase their knowledge base (often over various facets of the business), sharpen key skills (e.g., critical thinking and reasoning skills, presentation skills, interpersonal skills, etc.) and develop important contacts within the company often through a rotating work schedule. If your company does not have such a program, or if you are unable to get into such a program, here is what you can do.

After having had the opportunity to review the skill sets of all of the various co-workers and colleagues with whom you interact with on a regular basis, attempt to identify a select few people whom can act as your corporate mentors. Similar to identifying and developing a relationship with someone of greater political capital in the company (corporate shepherd), you should also seek to identify and develop relationships with those who possess the specific knowledge base and skill set that can directly and positively influence you and your competency level.

Be selective in who you chose to personally designate as your mentors. Unlike selecting an appropriate shepherd however, your mentor does not necessarily need to have a wealth of political capital within the organization. What is important is how much they know about what you wish to learn.

Here a few tips on selecting and using a mentor:

- You must identify exactly what it is that you wish to learn. You must know where you would like to see yourself in the near future. Refer to your 1, 3 and 5 year plans for assistance here. Identify a specific area of the organization, a specific department, a specific position, and tailor you mentor selections around those individuals with the knowledge base in your target area.

- Don't equate the lack of political capital with the lack of knowledge when selecting an appropriate mentor. One might have an extensive understanding of a particular discipline; however, might not have been successful in leveraging that knowledge into political capital. In selecting and developing a mentoring relationship, "what they know" is more important than "who they know."

- Consider their personality. Someone with a wealth of knowledge will not truly benefit you unless they possess a pleasant and engaging personality. You can test the waters here with a few simple questions that you pose to them about relevant topics. If you get the sense that they do not have the time to share their ideas or thoughts with you or are not giving you the time and attention that you are looking for, try someone else. As strange as it may sound, there are people out there who do take great satisfaction and fulfillment in helping assist and develop younger people. Try to find someone who truly takes joy in assisting and guiding less experienced employees.

- Consider the frequency and the manner in which you have regular contact with them. Someone based in an out of state location might be able to trade an occasional phone call or email with you; however, if you are looking for someone you can personally meet with on a more frequent basis, you might consider someone at your office location.

- Consider external mentors. When all else fails, if you cannot find a legitimate mentor at your company or at your location, try joining some related trade organizations. At the organizational meetings, try searching the membership for a legitimate mentor.

- Try to be somewhat selective in your solicitation for assistance. You must recognize that your mentor has a job to do themselves, and you must respect the fact that what they are doing for you is out of the goodness of their heart, and not necessarily an obligation. As such, try not to over burden your mentor with excessive inquiries or inquiries about insignificant items. Be selective.

- Offer a sincere thank you occasionally. After you have identified your mentor and developed a favorable relationship, be sure to let them know how grateful you are for their assistance. A sincere "thank you", or a small gift during the holidays, can go a long way and can often be sufficient to sustain a strong mentor / student relationship for a long time.

Learn How To Work A Room

In an earlier tip we discussed the importance of attending corporate events as a way of exhibiting your commitment to the organization; however, we also discussed the fact that these events are also used by management as fishbowl to observe how some of their younger professionals handle themselves in social settings. Therefore, young professionals must learn to develop and master certain social skills that will enable them to succeed in these settings. Anyone who has ever attended a corporate cocktail party and dinner of some kind knows what I am referring to here. There are those individuals who are visibly uncomfortable in such settings, often clutching their drink in one hand and standing alone off in a corner somewhere. Then there are those individuals who are completely at ease in approaching groups of individuals, whom they have never met before, carrying on an interesting conversation, closing the conversation and moving onto other individuals in the room. Watching someone who has mastered the art of truly working a room is almost like watching poetry in motion. It seems to me that the primary difference between these two different types of people is that the person who has mastered the skill of social networking actually and truly enjoys meeting different people and hearing what they do, what their backgrounds are, what their opinions are, etc. They do not see it as work. They see it as real fun. They truly and sincerely find joy in meeting new people. The person standing off in the corner is often thinking to himself, "What if I don't have anything to say?", "What if I can't contribute anything meaningful and interesting to the conversation?", "What if I look like an idiot?", etc. Those who are not at ease in such social settings see these events as uncomfortable and uninteresting. A great way to start improving your ability to adapt to such a setting is simply to adopt the right attitude.

Young professionals need to practice the intricacies of social networking. Here are some basic tips:

- View social networking as something fun and enjoyable, and you are more likely to lose your nerves. Try making a game out of it with your co-worker. When at a social event, agree to meet up in an hour or so and see who collects the most business cards from other guests.

- Smile. No one likes talking to someone who looks angry, frustrated or uneasy.

- Be brave. When you find it difficult to approach someone, try thinking to yourself that this person might be the one person who has the power to dramatically influence my career, my earnings, my future, etc. Consider what you have to gain if you do approach them, and consider what you may never know if you don't.

- Be sincerely inquisitive. If you are having difficulty contributing anything to the conversation try asking the other person questions about himself or herself, their occupation, their experiences, etc. Most people enjoy talking about themselves.

- Use appropriate humor occasionally. As an inexperienced young professional, try using some lighthearted humor when approaching a guest. Try opening the conversation with something like "Good evening, my name is _[Name]_ and I'm with _[Company]_, this is my first real networking event and I am as nervous as a turkey on Thanksgiving Day, do I look like it?" A light opening like this is sure to get a laugh from your counterpart and provides for a great entrée into a larger topic such as how to handle such events. Who knows, your counterpart in the conversation may even decide to put you at ease by introducing you to all of his or her colleagues in the room. Together they might all provide you with their best advice on how to handle these types of social settings.

- Do not order an alcoholic beverage unless your boss orders one first. And then, never have any more than one drink. Stay sharp!

Always Bring a Pad and Pen To A Meeting...And Use Them

When you are called to a meeting, be sure that you always bring a pad and a pen with you. I cannot tell you how many times I have seen a young professional attend a meeting with absolutely nothing in their hands. Walking into a meeting empty handed appears as though you do not anticipate any meaningful information or instructions to be discussed, which is disrespectful to the host. It also appears as though you are unprepared. As a young professional, simply having a pad and pen with you when called to a meeting is courteous and appropriate, regardless of how short or long the meeting or how significant or insignificant the topic. Having a pad and pen with you when called to a meeting will also prove invaluable when your boss rattles off a lengthy list of tasks for you to complete.

You should also make some efforts to jot down some notes throughout the meeting. Whether or not you actually will require the notes later on is insignificant. The act of taking notes is a visual confirmation that you are attentively listening to the speaker and that you value the information that they are sharing.

Think In Terms of Dollars

The almighty dollar feeds the insatiable appetite of corporate America. Companies are always searching for new ways to enhance profitability. Greater profitability allows a company to increase its capital position and thus devote greater resources toward research and development, product enhancements, marketing, employee training and development, acquisitions of assets and so forth, all of which will ultimately help to strengthen the financial condition and competitive position of the company. As a young professional, you must understand the importance of this concept. Throughout your day-to-day responsibilities, you should constantly be searching for potential profit-enhancing and cost-saving opportunities within your position, group, division and organization. In fact, the number one task on all job descriptions in all of corporate America should be "Identifies and implements revenue enhancing and cost reduction initiatives."

If you think you have found a way to save your company money, do your homework before you present your idea to your boss. Speak with some of your close colleagues in the office and ask them for their thoughts. You may find that the idea had already been suggested by someone else, but never implemented for a certain reason (e.g., too expensive, too time consuming, not in accordance with the company's mission, etc.). You may find that your proposed solution overlooks a key piece of information or contains a significant flaw. Be sure that your idea is feasible and reasonable. By that, I mean that it is not cost prohibitive and could be implemented with relatively little difficulty and its value can be truly justified. Casually speak with members in each of the major functional areas of the organization that affect your idea, and ask them about your idea.

After you have done your due diligence, if your idea still makes sense, prepare a formal study on the proposal. Try performing an analysis of your idea to see how much money the proposal can save the company. For instance, if you notice that account representatives generally book airfare and hotels to see their clients each year only two weeks in advance, but that they generally visit the same clients the same time each year, maybe suggest having these trips booked three to six months in advance. Lets assume your group has 25 account reps, each with 50 clients, and this proposal could save approx. $200 on each trip, this equates to an estimated annual savings of $250,000!

It may be that your proposal does not even necessarily save the company any money, but rather utilizes resources more effectively, to allow for greater efficiency or effectiveness. For instance, assume you work with a staff of service personnel who are supposed to spend their time out in the field addressing certain issues with clients (e.g., product training, repairs, maintenance, etc.). It soon becomes clear to you that a significant amount of their time is consumed by the various reports that need to be prepared once they return from the field. Perhaps you might identify a way to significantly streamline this reporting process so as to allow the service personnel more time in the field serving their clients. This proposal does not necessarily save the company any money, but it does certainly enhance the value of the process by identifying a method that better utilizes existing resources (e.g., service personnel out in the field more), strengthens customer service quality and builds client loyalty.

Before presenting your idea, just be sure to think through the suggestion thoroughly. Chart a workflow diagram and make certain that you fully understand the existing process and exactly how your proposed solution would function. Quantify your findings in terms of dollars and cents. If you can easily quantify how much money your idea will save the company, do so. If your idea does not necessarily save your company any money, try to quantify the "value" that your idea will create to the company. Using our previous example of the service personnel, assume that an average service member is paid $35,000 per annum. Assuming that they make an average of 100 service calls a month. This equates to an average salary cost of $29.17 per service call ($35,000 / 12 Months = $2,917 / 100). If your idea allows the service personnel to stay out in the filed longer and therefore increase their average service calls to 115 per month, the average salary cost for a service call falls to $25.37, a 13% increase in value. If you have 15 service personnel, that are now each making approximately 115 calls per month at an average cost of $25.37 per call, this equates to an estimated value enhancement of $78,660. This value doesn't even begin to quantify any of the added value by way of the improved customer service and stronger brand that you will be creating for your customers.

Once you are fully satisfied with your logic, your recommendation and your calculations, present the idea to your boss in a written format and offer to meet with them at their convenience. If your boss likes it, offer to assist them in any way possible to communicate and implement the idea. The central theme here is to constantly think to yourself in terms of dollars and cents. How can I enhance revenues for the company? How can I reduce costs? How can I do the same in less time? How can I do more with the same resources?

Do Not Use Your Company Email Account And Internet Access For Personal Use

While it is usually stated in your employer's policies, many employees often forget that their company email account is the sole property of their employer. Policies typically state that such accounts should not be used for personal use and are only to be used for legitimate business purposes. The nature of such restrictions is geared, in part, toward maintaining productivity amongst its employees. Employees simply should not be spending company time trading emails with friends and family. However, these restrictions are also critical to maintaining the integrity of the company's computer networks by preventing the spread of destructive computer viruses and unauthorized database intrusions. Such viruses can wreak havoc on the smallest and largest of companies. Eliminating such viruses often requires extraordinary efforts among the company's information and technology personnel and can often cost a significant amount of money to resolve. In light of these concerns, many companies have established strict internal policies regarding the use of company email accounts. Additionally, many companies closely monitor the content and subject matter that is transmitted via company email accounts. Today's advanced control and monitoring applications have made this rather easy and inexpensive to do.

In certain companies, it may be readily accepted that employees use their email accounts for personal use; however, consider the implications to your reputation and your career at that company if you should be the one who unintentionally downloaded the latest version of a highly disruptive computer virus, which completely destroys the company's databases. With the aforementioned monitoring software available today, your employer will know that the virus was introduced to their networks from your company email account.

My advice to all young professionals when it comes to using their company email account is as follows:

- Become familiar with your company's security policy with respect to your company email account and internet access.

- Do not provide your company email address to your friends or family members.

- If your friends or family members do send you personal emails to your company email account, ask them to refrain from doing so again.

- You should always be guided by your company's email security policy; however, a good rule of thumb is not to open any email where you do not recognize the sender. Call your manager or your information and technology department for assistance.

Be Careful With Referrals

Hiring the right people in the right positions is essential to the success of any organization. Today's hiring practices are much different than they were 20 or 30 years ago with the growing use of certain evaluation techniques such as competency tests, personality tests, honesty tests, drug tests, etc. However, despite all of these highly precise measurement and evaluation techniques, many companies still place a great deal of weight on the "referral" of a candidate from a respected employee of the organization. Some may argue that the endorsement of a certain candidate from a valued and reputable member of the organization is of the utmost importance. I am certain that we have all heard the saying "It's not what you know, it's who you know."

Hiring employees through the use of employee agencies and/or professional recruiters can be excessively expensive. Thus, many companies today offer financial incentives to its employees for referring candidates for open positions. If hired, incentives for referrals can be rather lucrative, especially to a young professional in the early stages of their career. This coupled with the prospect of having the opportunity to work next to your fraternity brother or best friend can, and often does, lead many of today's young professionals to recommend their friends for open positions in their places employment.

While this is not necessarily something that should be prohibited entirely, it is important for the young professional to understand the implications and consequences of referring someone they know to their human resource department. In essence, by you referring them to your employer, you are essentially giving them your stamp of approval that they are competent, capable and hard working. Young professionals must know that if they refer someone for an open position, and that person is hired, the success or failure of that person can be traced back to you. If your referral ends up being a "dud", a "slacker" or an "idiot" some may question your sense of judgment. More importantly, if your referral ends of being accused of any wrongdoing (e.g., theft, harassment, etc.), some may question your connection to that individual and thus, bring into question your own character and morals. My thoughts have always been that young professionals should not refer personal friends or family to their employer. However, referring someone who is professionally associated with you (e.g. former co-worker) who has demonstrated a clear competency level and an admirable work ethic over an extended period of time is, on occasion, acceptable.

Bite Your Tongue

As a professional, you have to learn how to restrain yourself from openly criticizing the culture, policies, procedures or practices of your co-workers, colleagues or employer. Open and excessive criticism of the status quo is dangerous, especially if you are a relative new comer and are in the early stages of your career. Those who routinely complain about or criticize the organization are not generally perceived as corporate loyalists. In many cases, employees who have little experience are not likely to be fully informed on the specific intricacies and mechanics of how processes, procedures or practices actually work. Given the absence of lengthy experience, in many cases, their complaints or criticisms may actually be totally unfounded.

At face value, it might be easy to say, "I can't believe that this company doesn't give its account representatives company cars to use." However, the employee may not understand the financial workings behind the company's policy. Awarding all of the company account representatives company cars to use could increase costs to the company (e.g., costs to purchase, repair, maintain, insure, etc.), therefore reduce profitability, and adversely affect any type of incentive based compensation (e.g., bonus) tied to profitability. Perhaps that may be the reason why the Company doesn't provide company cars.

You must be very cautious about the extent and the openness of any "water cooler" talk where you and your co-workers are criticizing your company or any of its employees. This does not, in any way, mean that you cannot comment on existing policies, procedures or practices. If you truly feel that there is a faster, cheaper, stronger or more efficient way to do something, be sure to do your homework first before criticizing the matter. Do your due diligence, research the issue, study the costs and the requirements of implementing your solution and present your idea to your boss in a diplomatic and professional manner.

Excessive criticism of your company's polices, procedures, practices or people is inappropriate, unprofessional and representative of an anti-company, anti-team attitude.

Know Your Industry

Having a firm understanding of your respective industry, your particular market, and its relevant rules, regulations and laws is essential. Senior management must have essential knowledge of the rules, regulations and laws that govern their industry and marketplace. Having similar knowledge at such an early part of your career can be used as a resourceful tool to truly distance yourself from your coworkers.

Inquire around your company about what state and federal agencies are responsible for regulating your company and its industry. Become familiar with these regulatory agencies and dedicate some of your efforts to understanding the respective regulations. Many regulatory agencies offer an email notification service where you can be automatically informed of any relevant regulatory changes or news events. Such notifications will inform you of any proposed regulatory changes, newly adopted regulations and other applicable regulatory news. These services are ideal and will aid you in developing an up to date knowledge of the regulatory environment in which you are operating. Have copies of these regulations in your desk or on your PC available for reference as needed. This knowledge can empower you to raise relevant issues to your manager as soon as possible. For instance, you might learn that a certain regulation is expected to change next month that would require the department to restructure a complicated process. With this knowledge you can address the issue with your boss to ensure that appropriate steps are being taken to comply with the new regulation.

I should note that when you do contact a senior member of your organization about a regulatory issue that you just learned of, you should always assume that they are as informed as you. Failing to do so may appear insulting by suggesting that they are not equally informed. Rather, present the issue to them in a manner that is diplomatic, respectful and resourceful. For instance, "Mr. Smith, I was just informed of the proposed changes to CFR 560.93. As you know, this change will greatly affect our existing procedures. If you require any assistance in developing an appropriate solution, I would be glad to assist you. Thank you."

This statement informs your manager that you are aware of the proposed regulatory change, and does so in a manner that assumes they are equally informed. The manner in which the message is delivered is a "Win-Win" for you. If your manager knows about the regulatory change, you are simply offering your assistance to them in developing an appropriate solution. If he or she does not know about the regulatory change, you will appear knowledgeable and informed, and arrive on scene as the hero of the day for not only notifying them about the regulatory change, but also offering your assistance to help.

Find a Friend in IT (Information and Technologies)

As a young professional you will be instructed or trained to perform certain tasks, and then will be expected to complete such tasks exactly as you were told. Young professionals seldom challenge an established process or the status quo. However, many young professionals fail to realize that identifying efficiencies within existing processes can greatly benefit them and their employer. Identifying such efficiencies will help distance the enterprising young professional from their peers and co-workers. Identifying such efficiencies will help develop the individual's reputation as a knowledgeable and competent employee. Identifying such efficiencies will also help to highlight the individual's ability to truly "think outside the box" and approach obstacles from diverse angles and varying perspectives.

One of the most important tools that can be used to uncover such hidden efficiencies is to evaluate the process or tasks relative to the technologies that are, or are not, being used to complete the tasks. In many cases, processes are not supported by the right technological application or are not making full use of the application. For instance, assume you are required to assemble a monthly report of some kind. In preparing such report you have been instructed to manually pull data from several different networks or applications, manually make certain mathematical calculations, present the data in a certain format and then issue copies of the report to various people. Given the intensity of manual inputs and lack of systems integration, it might take you several hours to assemble this report as you were instructed. However, you might find that you can create a pre-formatted template spreadsheet that, on a certain date and/or time, can be programmed to pull the required data from the various sources and applications, automatically perform the necessary calculations, and automatically email the report to a pre-established distribution list. If you can successfully develop a template format, program it to capture the necessary data and automatically distribute it, you might find that this task now takes you a matter of seconds, rather than hours. This will allow you to focus your time on other tasks, which will further increase your value to the group.

There are a great many of opportunities such as this example that are likely hidden in your day-to-day responsibilities. You may have a idea on how to streamline a specific task; however, you might not necessarily have the technological and systems background to fully understand what types of technology solutions might be available, and how feasible such solutions may be in your particular case. As such, you should seek to identify an appropriate person in the company's information technology group and strategically develop a relationship with them. Approach them, introduce yourself and tell them what your role is within the company. Indicate that you are attempting to evaluate a certain problem and would greatly appreciate some technical advice. Offer to buy them lunch at their favorite restaurant on a day that is most convenient for them. Workload and schedules permitting, often you will find that people are more than gracious about sharing their knowledge or offering their assistance when a colleague asks for it. Once you have established a date or time to meet, prepare for the meeting accordingly. Utilize the luncheon, the meeting or the conversation efficiently. Know exactly what you want to say and what you want to ask. Lay out your problem for them quickly, precisely and clearly. Using diagrams to illustrate your problem or obstacle is a helpful way to communicate your thoughts on what you are trying to accomplish. Prepare your diagrams, questions and thoughts ahead of time so that you can get the information you need as fast as possible and do not become a burden on the other person's schedule.

Be sure to sincerely thank that individual for their time and advice. Depending upon how extensive or involved they were in assisting you, you might even wish to send a follow up email or phone call once again expressing your gratitude for their assistance. This is important since you never know when you may again need some technical advice. A sincere "Thank You" will go a long way toward preserving what could be a very valuable relationship for you and your career.

Keep A Record of Your Objectives and Accomplishments

As a young professional you need to think about the way your position affects your department, and the organization as a whole. Think about how you can improve the efficiency or effectives of your job or other related functions. You should constantly be assessing your role within the group and devising methods to enhance your value to the group. As you identify, research, solicit and implement your ideas, it is critical that you keep a detailed record of all of your accomplishments. You should keep a detailed record of the things that you would like to accomplish (objectives), as well as a list of the things that you have achieved (accomplishments).

Every few months, you should update your list of objectives adding to it new objectives that you wish to undertake, as well as to report the progress made on your "in progress" objectives. Similarly, you should also update your list ever few months to memorialize those objectives, which have been realized and completed. Your objectives should be job related, but above and beyond your standard duties and responsibilities. For instance, if your job description calls for you to prepare certain management reports each month, this task is part of your job, and you are clearly expected to perform it. Simply completing this task each month will not add any value to you, because it is what you are expected to do based upon the parameters of your job description. However, if you identify a more efficient or more accurate method of preparing these reports, that is an example of something that you would have accomplished that was above and beyond your standard duties and responsibilities.

Developing a written list of all the objectives that you would like to achieve each year also gives some order, purpose and direction to your efforts, and allows you to focus your attention on specific tasks. While you will certainly need to attend to all of your day-to-day responsibilities each day, you should also find time to refer to this list each day so as to provide you with some clarity regarding your long term purpose and direction within the group and organization.

Establish a strategy or action plan on how you expect to achieve each objective. Assign specific deadlines to each objective. Failure to assign a specific deadline to an objective will inevitably delay its completion. Fully commit yourself to meeting these self-imposed deadlines, and assign regular checkpoints along the way to ensure that you are progressing as expected. Also, try to assign a priority level to each objective. This will help you to focus your earliest and greatest attention on those objectives that will have the greatest impact on your position, department, group or company. To give you some extra incentive on achieving such objectives, assign a specific and personal incentive to each accomplishment (e.g., buy yourself a new outft, a weekend getaway with friends, etc.).

In addition to keeping a written record of the objectives that you expect to achieve in the upcoming year, be sure to keep a written record of all of the objectives that you achieved over the last year (accomplishments). These accomplishments may or may not have been on your list of intended objectives. These accomplishments may have been attained intentionally or unintentionally. These accomplishments could be anything from a process that you improved, costs that you helped reduce, errors or inaccuracies that you uncovered, personnel that you trained or developed and so forth. Again, your list of accomplishments should include only those items that are considered to be above and beyond your standard duties and responsibilities.

Write down when you achieved each objective, as well as the impact that this will have on the group and the company. When at all possible, attempt to quantify the value of each accomplishment into dollars and cents. This will add substance to your achievements. For instance, if you are required to perform a certain task each week that requires about 2 hours of your time each week, and you successfully found a more efficient method that only requires 1 hour of your time each week to do the same task. Calculate the value of this new and improved method. For instance, if you are earning $52,000 per annum, your weekly salary is $1,000 per week or $25 per hour (based upon a 40 hour work week). As such, you were being paid $50 per week or $2,600 per annum to perform this one specific task. Your new and improved process, which reduced the time required to complete this task by 50% ultimately enhanced your value to the company by $25 per week or $1,300 per annum. Since you would have been paid your full salary anyway regardless of the new process, you may not necessarily have "saved" your company any money; however, your more efficient process did enhance your value as it now allows you to focus more attention on other tasks and responsibilities that you would not have had the time to do so under the old process, which therefore increases your value. Keeping a written list of your accomplishments also informs and alerts a young professional about what they have or *have not* accomplished throughout the year. Many of us are all too easily caught up in the day-to-day responsibilities of our job; we often fail to reflect on what it is that we actually accomplished each day, week, month, year, etc.

Keeping a written record of these accomplishments will ensure that you stay on track to achieving your true long-term objectives.

When it comes time for your performance evaluation, it is critical that you discuss with your manager all of your accomplishments. He or she may not be fully aware of each of your accomplishments; thus, it is your responsibility to ensure that they are truly informed.

To summarize, here are the key points to tracking your objectives and accomplishments:

- Each year, develop a list of all of the objectives that you would like to achieve,

- Be sure that these objectives are job related, and above and beyond your standard duties and responsibilities,

- Assign a priority level to each objective, and work on the most important objectives first,

- Develop a strategy or action plan for how you expect to achieve each objective,

- Assign deadlines for each objective, and establish appropriate checkpoints throughout the year to gauge your progress,

- Keep a written record of all of the accomplishments that you successfully achieved throughout the past year, including both intended and unintended accomplishments,

- Try to quantify the impact of your accomplishments in terms of dollars and cents,

- When appropriate, be sure that your manager is well aware of all of your achievements, particularly when it is time for your performance evaluation.

Publicize Yourself

Try to find creative, yet discreet, methods for publicizing yourself throughout the group and organization. The more so-called publicity you can provide for yourself the easier it will be for people to recognize your name, even when they may never have met you. The only real challenge is to make sure that management perceives the manners you opt to utilize to promote yourself in a positive context. You should not seek to promote yourself in a manner that is too obvious, inappropriate or unprofessional. For instance, you shouldn't seek to promote yourself throughout the group by way of consistently taking credit for completing tasks and assignments that are an innate part of your responsibilities and you shouldn't seek to promote yourself throughout the group by way of insignificant or failed projects, which have little or no value to the group. Find meaningful, material and resourceful methods for promoting your name and your abilities. Listed below are a few examples:

- Include your name, title and phone extension as "Prepared By" on relevant reports, spreadsheets or other such correspondences that you prepare, which are intended to be circulated to management. This will not only allow anyone with a question on the data to contact you, but will also act as "free advertising" to senior members of the group who receive the report. If they meet you at a cocktail party and hear your name, they are more inclined to say "Oh yes, you prepare the month end divisional sales report for us, don't you?" From here you have an opening to a larger conversation with that manager. This also shows that you are willing to take true ownership in your work.

- As you commence a new job or new position try issuing a brief statement / bio to all of your relevant co-workers and colleagues expressing your enthusiasm at your new responsibility. Without including a formal resume' and without sounding as if you are "tooting your own horn" try including a brief overview of your educational background (e.g., alma mater, graduate work, etc.), relevant technical skills (e.g., knowledge of certain software applications, programming capabilities, etc.), a brief overview of your previous professional experiences (e.g., where you were before your new position and what your responsibilities were), a listing of all trade related organizations and groups that you belong to and a brief statement about some basic personal information (e.g., where you reside, whether you are married, whether you have any children, etc.).

Companies often publish newswires with such information for higher-level executives; however, rarely do so for lower level employees. Until you reach the point in your career where your employer's human resource or marketing department does this for you, you can facilitate a similar effort yourself. This is an easy and effective way for you to effectively introduce yourself to all of your new co-workers and colleagues. In your correspondence, be sure to express your excitement at this new opportunity and welcome the opportunity to meet all of your co-workers and colleagues at their conveniences. Include you phone extension and email so recipients can contact you if they wish to welcome you to the group or want to meet you personally.

- Consider coordinating a series of regular "lunch bag" roundtable discussions. These are open and informal forums that discuss relevant issues or challenges affecting many of the department's members. These forums are great opportunities that allow for the free exchange of thoughts, ideas and ultimately solutions on various topics. Many times, seasoned members of the organization who have considerable first hand experience in dealing with the topic at hand are often invited to the meetings to share their thoughts, ideas and experiences on the subject. So as not to interfere with everyone's schedule or productivity, the forums are typically held during lunchtime, hence the name "lunch bag" roundtable discussions. The forum usually identifies a topic (e.g, improving communication between the research & development and manufacturing groups) and is open to all applicable members who wish to contribute to the open discussion. These forums are informal and open discussions on relevant topics affecting the group. While the advantages of holding these forums are extensive, someone must take the initiative to coordinate the forums. Someone must select appropriate topics, prepare an applicable agenda, select a date and time, reserve the necessary accommodations (e.g., conference room, white board, projector, etc.) and invite all the members. In many cases, someone also has to take charge of the meeting to ensure that the discussion stays active and on point. Stepping forward to take charge of arranging and hosting such forums can be a great way to promote yourself within the group. Furthermore, management may very well become aware that you have taken the initiative to coordinate such forums. If so, you are likely to be viewed in a positive and productive context as having taken the initiative to facilitate shared knowledge, enhance group capacities and solve relevant problems.

Display a Conversation Piece

A very important ingredient to corporate success is your ability to develop appropriate professional relationships within the organization. These relationships can be in the form of a close colleague whose assistance or opinion you can always rely upon when needed, an information and technology guru whose expertise is invaluable, a prominent executive who carries significant political capital, and so forth. For most young professionals, the challenge in developing these relationships is the initial encounter where an impression is formed and an opinion is made about the young professional. Employees working in separate departments or divisions of the organization may never have the opportunity to meet, particularly if there is no underlying business reason to the encounter. However, some reasonable efforts can be made to encourage and facilitate such encounters. It is within these initial encounters that names, titles, backgrounds and experiences can be briefly exchanged between the two parties so as to establish a connection of some kind, regardless of how formal or informal.

A simple and often effective means to encourage such encounters is to display some type of a unique conversation piece at your workspace. An item that catches someone's eye, strokes their curiosity and leads them to question the nature of the item can be helpful in fashioning an encounter with someone who may be of some significant value to you and your career. A baseball signed by a major league MVP, a mind twisting puzzle that beckons someone to try to solve it, a rare collectible or a captivating photograph are all good examples of things that might strike peoples interest causing them to stop by and strike up a discussion.

I do caution young professionals not to over decorate their workspace. Your workspace is meant for work and should not be cluttered with voluminous personal artifacts. Also, be particularly cautious that the item is appropriate for display at the office, does not reflect poorly upon you or create controversy of any kind. My general advice is to refrain from displaying religious, political or other types of items that could stir emotions or cause controversy. For instance, if your CEO or other members of the executive team are steadfast members of the Democratic Party, it's probably not smart to display a picture of you with a nationally recognized Republican politician.

Additionally, since the item is intended to be a "conversation" piece, you must be prepared to discuss the item with someone when they ask you about it. You should be prepared to discuss where you found it, why you are interested in the item (e.g., hobby, family keepsake, etc.), what the item represents to you (e.g., Does the item have any symbolic value to you?) and so forth.

Bring In Bagels and Doughnuts

People are often influenced by the smallest and most insignificant gestures. It's amazing how the littlest things can go such a long way in building your rapport with your co-workers and developing meaningful relationships within the group. If you don't believe me, try brining in a bunch of bagels or a bag of doughnuts for all of your co-workers to enjoy once in a while. Since many of us often rush out of the house in the morning trying to beat the traffic or catch the train, breakfast is a meal that is all too often skipped by many of us. For anyone who has found themselves in such a predicament, there are few things more pleasing than walking into the office and finding a bag full of fresh baked bagels or an assortment of doughnuts. As inconsequential and as trivial a gesture as this might seem, people can be influenced through actions such as these. Bringing in an occasional bag of bagels might not be sufficient to coerce your co-workers into joining you in the office next Saturday to help you finish a time sensitive project that you are working on. However, simple and discreet gestures such as these serve to illustrate your thoughtfulness and appreciation for your co-workers, which will help to form a foundation of support within the group with which you can further build upon.

A word of caution however, is not to overdo your efforts to express your thoughtfulness and kindness to your colleagues. Excessive and extraordinary gestures may appear phony and insincere. For instance, bringing in bagels and doughnuts should not be a regular occurrence, but rather an occasional surprise. Additionally, don't overdo the magnitude of your gift. For instance, as much as your co-workers appetites may very well appreciate the gesture, it might not be smart to hire a personal chef with their own omelet bar to come to your office and serve you and your co-workers tailor made omelets, waffles or pancakes. Be mindful of how you may be perceived if your gestures are too extravagant and lavish. The message you are attempting to convey is your kindheartedness toward and appreciation of your co-workers and colleagues. This message can easily be lost if the means in which it is communicated is so extreme or unusual.

Turn The Personal Cell Phone Off

While in the office, turn your personal cell phone off. Most companies have some form of a restriction or policy on using the office telephones for personal use. While there are certainly cost considerations to this, many of these restrictions and policies were also developed from a perspective of wishing to preserve productivity. Excessive personal use of the office telephones will adversely affect employee productivity. While using your own personal cell phone doesn't cost your company anything, doing so on company time is inappropriate and an ineffective use of company time. While you may be a professional, and you may be entitled to an occasional personal phone call, the fact of the matter is that while you are at the office, during office hours, you should not be engaged in routine personal conversations with your family or friends. This is especially true early in your career as you are attempting to develop a reputation for yourself and striving to build some political capital. Moreover, with the endless supply of customized ring tones that are now available, it is becoming increasingly more annoying to others in the office, to have to listen to someone else's phone ring the theme of the latest movie soundtrack or top 40 hit.

Stay Current On Events

Stay current on relevant issues in the news. Simply watching the six o'clock news each night, or reading a daily tabloid news publication just will not keep you as informed as you need to be throughout your career. Typically, such media will only cover the ratings grabbing stories and often fail to report on broader and deeper subjects. Even when more pertinent topics are covered they are rarely covered in sufficient detail to truly educate someone on the true nature of the event.

To stay current on relevant issues, you must read a nationally recognized and reputable newspaper such as the New York Times or The Wall Street Journal. The valuable information that you will obtain will provide you with sufficient knowledge and information about a wide array of topics that will aid you in engaging in and contributing to spontaneous discussions with your manger, senior manager or clients. Be sure to make such reading a daily part of your schedule.

Often when you least expect it (e.g., ride in an elevator, walking out of the building, a short break in between meetings, etc.), conversations may be started, some business related, and some having nothing to do with business at all. In many cases, these conversations may pertain to relevant events or issues in the news. To appear informed and educated, you need to be able contribute to such discussions. Contributing additional information about a pertinent story in the news that is being discussed will aid you in enhancing your reputation as a knowledgeable, well-versed and worldly individual.

Just remember to be cautious about expressing your personal opinion on politically and socially sensitive issues. Contributing additional information that is factual and based upon a reliable and reputable source is acceptable. However, try to refrain from expressing your own personal feelings and opinions on highly emotional and politically charged issues, which takes us to our next tip.

Stay Away From Non-Business Hot Button Issues

As you start your career and attempt to build a solid and favorable reputation for yourself, you need to focus your efforts on working harder, working smarter and working faster than anyone else does. As much as you may wish to believe that this will be sufficient enough to prove yourself to your manager and advance your career, the fact of the matter is that other non-business items and events could potentially shape your manager's opinion of you and your professional capabilities. Things that you might say, beliefs that you might have and the manner in which you present them to others can easily shape one's opinion of you. While your work ethic and your overall performance are key considerations to be taken into account by your manager, many managers are also easily influenced, whether consciously or subconsciously, whether rightly or wrongly by their own personal opinion of you as an individual.

As an extreme example, assume you are an absolute star performer in the office, capable of out performing, out thinking and out hustling your co-workers. Then, assume for a moment that your boss decides to buy you and your co-workers a drink after work to celebrate a recent success. This one drink turns in to two, and two turns into three, and so forth. Before the night is over, you are dancing on the bar and singing a less than acceptable rendition of your favorite song. Having witnessed such as spectacle, it is quite possible that your boss will have a different opinion of you the next morning in the office.

Therefore, not only do you need to act in a certain way to ensure that your favorable reputation is preserved, but you need to be cautious about creating any unnecessary adversity or division within the office or the company. In other words, be careful about raising issues that are likely to raise one's emotions, where there is no obvious business related purpose. For instance, stay away from highly passionate and emotional topics such as politics and religion. Not knowing the full background, experiences and beliefs of your manager, co-workers or colleagues, its best not to engage in such politically charged "hot button" discussions in the office.

Assume for a minute that you are wholeheartedly against the war in Iraq, and happen to mention so in a political discussion that takes place within the office. Now assume that your manager, who may have overheard the discussion, had a son or daughter who lost their life in Iraq while serving in the military. While some managers may be very successful at distancing their personal beliefs and values of their employees from their professional opinions, there are many managers who may have some difficulty in doing this.

Young professionals are clearly entitled to their opinions, and are free to express them. However, in the context of a working environment, it is essential that young professionals be aware of the potential impact some of their beliefs and values may have on others in the office. Like it or not, one's personal values and beliefs are often taken into consideration as judgments are made and opinions are shaped about that person. Therefore, it is best to avoid displaying values or beliefs that carry with them deep and passionate emotions.

Sharpen Your Public Speaking Skills

Anyone who has witnessed an impressive, persuasive and motivating speaker knows the impact that a strong set of public speaking skills can have on how someone is perceived by others. Due to their inexperience and lack of practice, many young professionals may be uncomfortable speaking to a room full of people; many may even dread the idea. Standing in front of a room full of intense looking and time pressed executives is enough to make most of us uneasy, especially young professionals with limited professional experiences and limited public speaking occurrences. However, true public speaking ability is a talent that is invaluable in supporting one's career. This talent is wide ranging in its applicability and reaches across all industries and markets. Whether you are a sales representative trying to make a sale, a civil engineer presenting your findings to your client or a computer programmer explaining the logic behind a specific code to your manager you must know how to present yourself confidently, clearly and professionally in a public setting.

Given that many young professionals have not had sufficient time, experience and practice in developing this essential skill it is important that they take it upon themselves to study this discipline. Young professionals need to prepare themselves for the surprise phone call from their manager or senior manager asking them if they can assemble a short presentation on the project that they have just finished. Young professionals can turn to a multitude of seminars, courses, textbooks, CD's or DVD's to help develop their public speaking abilities. If you do not have the time or money for such resources try preparing various theoretical presentations. Then practice them whenever you have time. After you are confident that you have the presentation down, try performing the presentation in front of your home video camera, so that you can review yourself from the audiences' perspective. Whenever possible, ask your closest friends or family to sit in and listen to the presentation. Play the video back and try to gauge their reaction. How did you appear, confident, nervous, unsure, etc? What made you appear so? Were you slouching? Did you have your hands in your pockets or were you using them to emphasize certain points? Were you making eye contact with your *imaginary* audience? Was your speaking clear, confident, audible and absent of all the proverbial "filler" words such as the ubiquitous "Ummm" and "Ahhh"? Were you speaking at the proper cadence, not too slow, not too fast? If anyone sat in on the presentation, or watched the video with you, ask them for their honest opinion. Take a pen and some paper and make a list of all the things that you did right and more importantly all the things that you did wrong. Then practice the presentation again, focusing more attention on those areas that you wish to improve. Do this exercise again and again and again, until you truly feel confident and comfortable. To help you better your skills, try focusing some time each day on watching how other people speak in public and how they present. There are a number of cable channels that routinely cover business, political or courtroom news stories where video can often be found of highly experienced professionals delivering a compelling message. Take your pad and pen and write down all the things that you like and dislike about those presentations, then try to work them into your own presentations. Practice these presentations regularly and you will be surprised at how quickly your public speaking skills will be developed.

Be Prepared To Sacrifice Some Time With Friends

Young professionals need to know how to balance the demanding burden of a new career with their own personal life. Few would argue against the critical importance of family, and let me be crystal clear on this; I am in no way suggesting the sacrifice of family relationships here. However, many young professionals who have recently graduated college have developed what I would call rather expansive social networks. These social networks can range from a select few "best friends", to a group of "fun to hang out with friends", to a couple of "friends of a friend", to a variety of mere "acquaintances."

Young professionals need to search within themselves and determine just how committed and dedicated they are to their new career. The greater the level of commitment and dedication, the greater the level of sacrifice they must make in other areas of their life. It's pure mathematics; there is only twenty-four hours in each day. In other words, time is a finite resource. If as a young professional, you wish to commit yourself to learning your profession, establishing a favorable reputation within your company, building political capital and developing a proven record of accomplishment, you will likely be required to think far outside of the standardized nine o'clock to five o'clock mindset.

I am not saying that you need to abandon all of your friends. I am simply saying that young professionals need to understand that they will likely be required to sacrifice some personal time, in order to focus on the demands of their career. The question then becomes, where do you find this additional time?

Many young professionals often have groups of friends, and sometimes several groups of friends, all of which demand a considerable amount of personal time and attention. Before your career, you might have worked out at the gym with Frank on Monday's and Tuesdays, played basketball with Dave on Wednesdays, played poker with Steve and Tom on Thursday nights, gone out with Bill and Joe on Fridays, played golf with John on Saturday's and watched football with all of the above on Sundays. If you are serious about your career, if you are serious about making a favorable and positive impression on management, if you are serious about developing important skills and talents as a professional then you need to understand that this will require a significant amount of that finite resource of yours; your time.

My suggestion would be to talk this over with your friends and let them know that your decision to work later and longer hours will affect how much time you can spend with them. Ask them to understand your decision. Chances are, they will, as many of them might be venturing off into their own careers, and facing similar challenges at the same time as you. Also, review the personal relationships that you have with each of your friends. If you are like most people, you have primary and secondary friends. You have the friends whom you trust and admire and have known for many years. These primary friends are the friends that you are likely to turn to in the face of adversity or challenge. These primary friends are members of your support network, and you should work hard to retain these relationships. However, you may also have a number of friends whom might not be as important to you as your primary friends. These secondary friends might be fun or enjoyable company, but you might not see them as often as your primary friends, you might not share similar interests or you might not fully trust them. At first, it is within this tier of secondary friends that most young professionals should look for additional time and attention that can be dedicated toward their careers. Is it truly necessary to have fifteen or more so called "best" friends? Can you truly and honest rely upon each of these friends for support and guidance in a time of need? Has this support ever truly been tested by real life experiences? Which of your primary friends share similar interests, values and beliefs as you? Which of your primary friends share dissimilar interests, values and beliefs as you? Look deep inside each of your personal relationships with each of your friends and determine who is truly important to you. This process will free up additional time, attention and efforts for you, which can then be redirected towards developing your skills, talent, reputation and career.

<u>Learn To Write Well</u>

When you are composing a written correspondence of any sort, regardless of how formal or informal the correspondence may be, poor spelling, incorrect grammar or punctuation and weak sentence structure can convey a very poor message to your reader. This message may be one of incompetence, carelessness or non-professionalism.

Many of us have some level of difficulty in preparing a properly structured and well-written letter, memorandum, report, email, *etc.* Given the broadening diversity of America's workforce and the many different languages that are spoken, an employee of foreign nationality may have graduated at the top of their class from a highly reputable business school, but might not necessarily have a firm command of the intricacies and mechanics of the English language.

The quality of a young professional's writing abilities may be construed by their managers, senior management or clients, whether rightly or wrongly, as a reflection of their overall capabilities. In view of this, it is crucial that young professionals pay particular attention to the quality of their writings. In many larger companies, senior management simply does not have sufficient opportunity to meet each employee personally. Therefore, the extent of an employee's exposure to senior management may rest solely upon the quality of their memorandums, reports, analyses and other such written documents that are sent to the attention of senior management. In such cases, senior management's opinion of these employees could rest largely on the quality of the employee's writings.

Some may even argue that the quality of one's writing abilities is just as important as the quality of their technical abilities. An employee may in fact have outstanding professional and technical capacities; however, if they are unsuccessful at properly communicating their thoughts, opinions and findings in a clearly written format, they will encounter significant challenges in convincing others of their outstanding technical abilities.

It is also important to mention here that young professionals need to employ the same writing standards to all email communications that would apply to traditional written correspondence. Thanks in part to text messaging and instant messaging many young professionals are now accustomed to highly abbreviated, almost indiscernible, forms of communication when corresponding through email. Young professionals must be sure to employ the same quality standards when drafting their emails as they would a formal letter or memorandum. The ubiquitous nature of email has made it such a widely accepted form of communication that it deserves the same respect and credibility as other forms of written communication.

Developing your writing abilities can be accomplished in many ways. First, you should assess the damage. Ask someone you trust, someone you know who has a firm command of the language and someone who has displayed strong writing skills to read some of your work. Tell them that you are interested in developing your writing skills and ask them for their honest assessment of your writing abilities. Ask them to be specific about the quality of your writings. Is the information presented in a clear, concise and consistent format? If not, what are the areas that need to be improved upon? Don't stop there. Try doing some homework on writing abilities and attend a local seminar or class on the topic. Try finding one that pertains particularly to the style of writing that best suits your work. Perhaps you might even suggest to your manager that it might benefit you to take such a course on behalf of the company. Not only will this be easier on your wallet, it will show your manager that you are proactive about confronting your weaknesses and are interested in developing your skills.

Never stop trying to improve upon this skill. Go to a bookstore and find some appropriate books pertaining to the subject. Keeps these books in your desk for reference when needed. Most software applications now have spelling and grammar checking features that will assist the user in identifying obvious errors. Use these features to your advantage; however, never rely solely upon them. There is absolutely no substitute for a good solid proofing of your work.

Be A Walking Advertisement

One of the best ways to improve your chances of success and get noticed is to work diligently at bringing in profitable business to your company. Even though you may not hold a sales position, this doesn't mean that you cannot be a salesperson for your company. Always be on the lookout for potential opportunities for your company. For instance, if you work at a commercial bank, and your friend's father runs his own company, ask how the company is doing, where it banks, whether or not they are happy with their banking relationship, etc. Discuss the latest products or services that your bank offers and how they are different than the competition. You might ask your friend if his dad has heard about the latest sweep account product at your bank or the latest cash management products. Imagine what the possibilities are if you are responsible for setting up a face to face meeting between your company and a potentially lucrative client, especially when your position has nothing to do with business development or sales?

However, if you are successful at introducing a prospective client to your company, you have to know when to step aside. You first need to decide whom to contact within the company about your potential client. I would suggest contacting your direct manager or supervisor, informing them of the circumstances surrounding the matter and ask them how they think you should proceed. Don't get too involved in the process, unless it is your official responsibility. Set up an appropriate introduction between your prospect and the appropriate person or people in your company. Ask those responsible for handling your lead to keep you informed of the ultimate outcome. Did it result in a sale? If not, why? Be sure to keep a record of how many referrals you make to the company and how many of those referrals ultimately resulted in a sale, so that you can go on record as having contributed to the company's financial success at your next performance evaluation.

In your perpetual quest to generate sales for your company, be sure that you always have a business card on you. You never know when you might meet a potential client, or someone who knows a potential client. When distributing your business cards, write your home number or personal cell phone number on the back of the card. This shows that you are seriously interested in hearing from them, and that you are willing to dedicate your personal time and attention to making certain that they are treated properly.

Don't Hold A Grudge

It is nearly certain that you will have certain confrontations or conflicts with some of your coworkers, colleagues and superiors. Handling multiple tasks, working under strict deadlines, competing for monetary incentives and having to deal with a variety of personalities will often converge at some point into a conflict of some sort with your team mates, coworkers and possibly even your boss. It's not a question of "if?" it is a question of "when?" Therefore, young professionals must learn how to move past such an encounter quickly and professionally so as to get back to the tasks at hand.

When faced with a confrontation of some form, it is important that you not lose your cool and that you do not get personal, "cheap" or "dirty" in your line of reasoning. Stay professional, rational, and respectful, and be prepared to fully support every one of your arguments with facts and examples. After stating your case, if a resolution has still not been reached, leave the ultimate verdict up to the most senior member of the organization who is involved in the dispute and then be done with it. Do not hold a grudge. Put the event in the past, don't dwell on it, don't talk about it and don't mope around the office for the rest of the day. Forget about it, and get back to your responsibilities. In other words, move on!

After an emotional and often angry encounter with someone that you work with and see on a regular basis, many may find this exceptionally difficult to do, particularly younger and less experienced employees who might not be familiar with such encounters. Young professionals must understand that your employer is not asking you to be close friends and best buddies with everyone that you work with each day. Your employer is asking you to do your job, and to do it well, irrespective of whether you like or dislike the people that you must work with and irrespective of the emotions at play. Managers and supervisors do not want to, nor do they have time to resolve personality disputes and petty disagreements between employees. Managers and supervisors are not trained referees, therapists or counselors. Managers, supervisors, and senior management, simply want results.

Being able to pull yourself up from a brief encounter with a coworker and promptly regain your focus on the task at hand including the ability to continue working with that person who you were just arguing with, will show your manager a significant degree of maturity and professionalism on your part. Doing so will also show them that you have control over

139

your emotions and can remain focused on the tasks at hand regardless of your emotions and the level of frustration that you are feeling. Doing so will show your manager that you are professional enough to work with people that you might not necessarily get along with on a personal level, and can still accomplish the defined objective.

Use A Briefcase

It sounds silly that using a briefcase could possibly help you advance your career. However, many of these tips are simply designed to give a certain appearance, create a certain perception or foster a certain image of yourself that is in accordance with professionalism, productivity and competence. Carrying a briefcase is amongst the easiest suggestions one can offer in this regard. Simply holding a briefcase as you enter and exit the office may very well imply that you are bringing work home with you, an implication that you are busy, personally committed to your responsibilities and willing to sacrifice some of your personal time to complete your professional tasks and/or assignments. On the contrary, an individual walking out of the office with nothing in their hands, except their car keys creates a visual impression that the individual is quite literally leaving their work behind and unwilling to bring their work home with them, which could potentially create the impression that you are uncommitted and lack true dedication to your responsibilities as a professional. Remember, if you wish to be perceived as a true professional, you need to foster an image of professionalism, and the image of a professional is one that takes their job, its responsibilities and its burdens seriously. In other words, you need to convince your superiors that you are willing to sacrifice some of your own personal time in order to meet their expectations of performance and productivity. Simply carrying a briefcase goes a long way to supporting this perception.

Don't spend a significant amount of money on the latest fashion or style of briefcase. If you are walking around with a $1,200 attaché it is likely that you will be doing yourself more harm than good by sending a message that you likely have a sizable disposable income and are in no need for that next raise or promotion. Buy a simple and affordable briefcase and be sure to make good use of it each day.

Use An Overcoat

Consider this picture. A up and coming young professional is just returning from a high powered meeting where he just experienced the finest hour of his career. He just "nailed" a presentation to senior management about a new idea that he had developed, and received much kudos for it. As he returns to his desk, he starts getting ready to leave the office on a cold evening. He brushes some dust off of his recently polished shoes, he buttons his neatly pressed suit jacket and he straightens his tie with the Windsor knot that he just recently learned how to tie. Then before leaving the office, he slips on an old, torn and stained, leather sports coat that looks as if it was used in an actual World War II battle. On the way out of the office, that employee happens to share the elevator with some of the senior managers he had just presented his idea to. Is it possible that some of those senior managers might have a slightly different opinion of this employee now? Why? Because of the employees unwillingness to dress in full accordance with what most senior managers may visualize a true professional to look like.

Looking professional is more than polished shoes, a suit and a tie. It is an image of respect and dedication. The way you look can be a representation of your abilities, a representation of your level of dedication to your position and a representation of your respect for the organization. If you do not dress in complete accordance with what your senior managers visualize a true professional to look like, you may have difficulty persuading them that you are a true professional.

Notwithstanding the fact that the aforementioned employee just succeeded at presenting a well received idea to senior management, the vision of that employee wearing what many might see as an inappropriate form of attire in the office might adversely affect the employee's image in the office. Some may consciously or subconsciously see this as somewhat of a disconnect between the employees abilities and their respect and appreciation for their position. For instance, consider for a moment, that immediately following that presentation some members of senior management were so impressed that they asked that young professional to join them that evening for dinner as they entertain some of the company's high profile clients. How do you think senior management might feel as they introduce that young professional as the newest up and coming member of the team while he is wearing a torn and stained leather jacket bearing the logo of his favorite sports team?

Young professionals have to understand that the way they dress and the way they act are representations of many things including their own abilities and capacities, their level of dedication and commitment to their position and its responsibilities, as well as their overall respect for the organization.

Again, you do not necessarily need to purchase a $1,000 camel hair custom fitted overcoat. Just be sure that the coat is professional, fits you well and is appropriate for the office. The same rules apply for all other related accessories. These accessories include without limitation to raincoats, umbrellas, hats, luggage, belts, belt buckles, handbags, scarves, gloves, etc. No matter what the item, just be sure that it is appropriate for the office and entirely professional.

Do Not Use a Personalized Screen Saver

Do not personalize your office computer by downloading a personalized screen saver. While many companies do have administrative controls that prevent their employees from installing their own personal screen saver, many do not. If your company has a standardized screen saver or company logo, use it and use it in accordance with company policy. Doing so shows that you respect the corporate protocol that has been established and that you are buying into the corporate mission and philosophy of the organization. Using a company endorsed screen saver shows that you respect your workplace and how it appears to others. Clients, senior management or other VIP's may be walking through the office on their way to a meeting, and should not be made privy to a virtual smorgasbord of personal tastes and preferences from the many employees whom they are passing in the office. By installing a personalized screen saver you run the risk of offending someone in your office and possibly appearing as somewhat defiant; not the message that you should be interested in conveying to your manager. Pictures of your pets, your favorite sports team logo, humorous jokes, political commentaries and the like are all best left for your home, not the office.

<u>Author Something</u>

Advancing your career and your position within the company depends heavily upon you ability to persuade your manager and senior management that you are knowledgeable about relevant topics concerning your company and the industry it operates in, and that you have relevant ideas on how to create added value for your company and its clients. Often in the course of completing your day-to-day assignments and responsibilities it is difficult to find the time to meet with your boss to discuss certain ideas or suggestions. Therefore you may need to try to find some alternative ways of communicating your competence and sharing your thoughts on certain matters. Authoring an article on an industry related topic that you have some knowledge of is great way to do this.

Using your own personal time, try authoring an article, white paper or text of some sort on the topic and submit it to various trade related publications or journals. Ask for their comments, and request their consideration for it to be published in an upcoming issue. This will accomplish several things.

- *Sanctioning of Your Idea.* By asking various trade publications to scrutinize your article, they will in some way actually be proofing and scrutinizing your idea(s). If they decide to publish your article, they will in some way actually be endorsing it. In other words, if the publication didn't think your idea had some merit, they would not publish it. If the trade publications do not decide to publish it, you should seek their feedback on why it is not being published and then try to revise the article or start a new article on a more popular or pertinent topic. In an effort to help you select an appropriate topic, you might first try contacting the top two or three relevant trade publications and inquire if they are looking for articles on any particular topics over the course of the next several months. This might help give you some guidance on where to focus your attention.

- *Illustration of Your Passion.* As a young professional, few are likely to be asked by their managers or supervisors to actually author a trade related article. More often than not, this is not something that would be expected of a young professional. Thus, by you choosing to dedicate a great deal of your personal time to a relevant professional topic speaks volumes about your passion for your position, your company or your industry. It speaks volumes about your desire to be viewed as a competent and credible professional in your company and your field of work.

- *Free Advertising.* The more you can do to get your name and ideas known throughout your company and your industry the easier it will be for you to develop a positive reputation, create valuable political capital and advance your career. Most publications will likely offer you an author's mention, which will publish your name, title and the name of your employer. This will serve as a form of free advertising for you and for your employer.

- *Develop Meaningful Industry Contacts.* By publishing a trade related article, your name, ideas and thoughts will be published throughout the industry, to those who subscribe to the publication. This might help to open meaningful doors and relationships to other key individuals within the industry at other institutions. These individuals can help fortify your framework of contacts including mentors, business referral sources, career counselors, future job prospects, etc.

I will leave you with two critical pieces of advice concerning this tip:

- *Seek Approval.* Prior to authorizing the publication to print your article, be sure that you obtain official approval from your employer to publish the material. There is a chance that your employer may not agree with your idea or concept or does not wish to reveal certain information contained in the article. Therefore, once the publication has indicated a desire to publish your article, ask the publication for an edited copy of the article, exactly as it would appear in the publication so that you can seek approval from your employer. Email this to your manager, and ask for their guidance on what the proper protocol is for approving the document for publication. The article may need to be reviewed by senior management, the company's marketing department and possibly even its legal counsel.

- *Work on Personal Time Only.* When you are preparing the article be sure that you are not working on company time or using company resources (e.g., PC, printer, etc.). Given that authoring such articles is not likely a part of your job description and day-to-day responsibilities, you should prepare it completely on your own personal time.

It's All in The Presentation

Many of the world's greatest chefs will admit that much of their focus is not only on the recipe or the ingredients of their famous dishes, but the presentation of the dish as well. The same logic holds true when submitting a written piece of work to your manager, such as a memorandum or report. Not only is the content important, but so is the format and presentation of the document. Have you ever witnessed someone who prepares a memorandum using all capital letters? Have you ever seen a memorandum where there are numerous different font styles, with no particular rhyme or reason to them? Have you ever read a report that had more spelling and grammatical errors than a second grader's homework? Regardless of the content of the document, what was your impression of the author of that document? Lazy? Careless? Illiterate? Unprofessional? All of the above?

After you have prepared your memorandum, letter, report, etc., review it at least twice. The first review should be for its content, clarity and factual accuracy, and the second review should be focused solely on the appearance and presentation of the document. I am hesitant to say whether one is more important than the other, but it is clear that one without the other can adversely affect your intended message and the reader's opinion of you. Therefore you should place considerable value in both the substance and the appearance of your work.

Following are some helpful tips to guide yourself when reviewing your document for its appearance and overall presentation:

- Be sure that your margins are all properly aligned and evenly spaced.

- Be consistent with your formatting. For instance:
    o If you are abbreviating by referring to five million dollars as "$5MM" in one paragraph you should not be referring to another figure later in the memorandum as "$5,000,000."
    o If you are going to round your figures, do so consistently throughout the entire document.
    o If you are carrying figures out to a particular decimal point, be sure to carry all figures out to the same decimal point throughout the entire document. Don't refer to one figure as $132,500.00 and another figure as $17,000.
    o When using symbols, apply them consistently. For instance, if you are referring to figures in dollars and refer to one

figure with a dollar sign, be sure that all other figures that represent dollars also include a dollar sign (e.g., $100,000 vs. 100,000).

o When communicating a date, do not refer to one date as 03/17/07 and then another date as July 12th, 2007.

- Be aware of acronyms and abbreviations. If you wish to use an acronym or an abbreviation, be sure that the first reference to the item is a full description of the word(s) then followed by parenthesis containing the appropriate abbreviation, which will be used later throughout the document to refer to that item. For instance, if you wish to abbreviate a company name from Standard Wholesalers and Distributors, Inc. as SWD, your first reference to the company should read "Standard Wholesalers and Distributors, Inc. (hereafter referred to as "SWD")." After this initial disclosure, you have established an understanding throughout the rest of your document what "SWD" refers to.

- If you are using a spreadsheet or table of some kind with numeric inputs, you should always right justify the figures so that the numbers are all properly aligned by decimal points. See below:

Right
$5,250,000.00
$725,000.00
$31,250,000.00

Wrong	
$5,250,000.00	
	725,000
$31,250,000.00	

- If your document is more than 1 page long, imbed the current and total pages into the footer of your document (e.g., Page 1 of 3). This way, if a page gets lost in transition somewhere or if the document gets separated somehow (e.g., photocopying, distribution, filing, etc.) the reader will clearly identify that the document is incomplete. This also allows your reader to determine how long the memo or report is from the front page.

- If your document is not confidential, and you are working off of a shared network consider imbedding the file name and path into the footer as well. This way, anyone who may need access to the document knows its location.

- Use a font style that is professional and preferably familiar to your company. If you are interesting in highlighting a particular section of text for some purpose, try using the same font but with an italicized or bolded overlay.

- Use spell checking software,

- Use grammar checking software,

- Always, personally proof the entire document before submitting it,

Take "Ownership"

What do I mean by take "ownership"? I am referring to the importance of holding yourself accountable for your actions and the results that you produce. I am referring to the need to understand the value in what you are doing and conducting yourself accordingly. Many young professionals might be upset about some of the administrative or clerical responsibilities that they may have at the office. However, it doesn't matter if you are sitting in an executive suite developing a strategic vision for the organization or if you are photocopying and distributing monthly management reports, employees must understand the value in what they are doing and treat their responsibilities seriously and professionally. Taking ownership in what you are doing transcends the complexity, sophistication or importance of each task. Young professionals who constantly take ownership in their work will always exert the same amount of effort and attention to an insignificant task as they would a significant task. They never drag their feet, they never let up and they never give a half-hearted effort.

I have often said that the primary difference between an *employee* and a true *professional* is not the quality of their education, it is not the extent of their professional experiences, it is not their job title and it is not the size of their paycheck. It is whether or not they consistently take "ownership" in what they are doing. A true professional is someone who commits themselves to seeing that the task they have been assigned is done right and is done in the best interests of the department and organization. A true professional is someone who takes responsibility for their actions, and never lays blame on others.

I should also point out that true ownership also transcends the limitations of job descriptions and specific responsibilities. In other words, taking ownership means to take hold of a problem or an obstacle and seeing it to resolution, whenever and wherever possible, even when it is not really your problem to begin with. Consider the two following examples, and form an opinion about which employee has taken true "ownership" of the situation.

A back office bank employee is sitting at their desk working on a task when their phone rings. On the other end of the phone is a customer who was mistakenly directed to this back office employee's phone, rather than the branch where they have their deposit accounts. The customer on the phone would like to know what their available balance is in their checking account. One employee handles the situation as follows:

> "I'm sorry, but you have reached the Accounting Department, let me transfer you to your branch, and someone there will be happy to provide you with that information. Please hold."

It sounds like this employee has handled the situation, doesn't it? Well, I guess that all depends on your perspective of what you consider taking *ownership* in your work to be. For instance, consider how the next employee handles the situation.

> "I'm sorry, but you have reached the Accounting Department. I recognize that you have already been misdirected once, so if you would like, I'd be happy to take your name and account number and get you the information that you need myself. Would you like me to do this, or would you like me to have someone from the branch contact you directly?"

The first employee simply hands the issue off to the branch. There is nothing necessarily wrong with this approach; however, given that the customer had already been misdirected once before, I can't imagine that they would be interested in being transferred again. The second employee takes true ownership of the problem. The accounting department employee makes the branch's problem, his problem. He offers to assist the customer himself, and doesn't worry about who's job it is to provide the information. The employee has successfully handled the situation by taking ownership of the problem.

Taking ownership in your job, even when it is not really your responsibility to do so, shows a tremendous amount of professionalism. It shows management that you are capable of seeing above and beyond the constraints of individual job descriptions, and that you are capable of viewing problems from more of a larger organizational perspective. In other words, in the aforementioned example, the customer who was inquiring about their checking account balance may have represented a very large and lucrative client for the bank. Whether you work in the accounting department or the branch, the salaries of all bank employees are paid through such lucrative clients; thus, it is in everyone's best interests to see that the client was provided with the requested information, and that they were satisfied with how their request was handled. That is "ownership."

Make Use of Appropriate Software

Using the right software to help you organize your calendar, prioritize tasks, manage projects, maintain your contacts, track sales prospects and keep appropriate records can give you a tremendous advantage. It is hard to believe that in this day and age, many people still do not take full advantage of the many software applications that are out on the market designed specifically to assist them in their day-to-day tasks. In fact, many of these types of applications are generally available through the in-house software suite provided by many companies. If your company does not have such a software application, find one that will suit your needs, obtain the appropriate specifications (e.g., hardware requirements, memory space needed, etc.) and seek the approval of your manager and the IT Department to install it on your office computer or laptop.

In its most basic form, you will likely need an application that will help you accomplish the following objectives:

• Organize your appointments.

• Maintain your contact database.

• Manage your tasks.

• Manage projects.

The application should allow you to set alarms in advance which will notify you of an upcoming meeting or a task that is due at a certain time in the future. The application should be able to attach appropriate records and files to each task or project including memorandums, reports, emails, etc. This will help you organize your data and retrieve appropriate records easily. The application should also allow you to set recurring appointments and tasks. This will ensure that you never miss that monthly staff meeting, which is held on the last Friday of every month at 9:00 am. Scheduling recurring tasks are also important as you can set a reminder each day, week or month to complete a specific task such as that month end or quarterly report that you manager has to have on time. Ideally, the contact database should also allow you to input information concerning the nature of each conversation that you have with your contacts. For instance, if you are speaking with a high profile prospect and learn something personal about them, such as their favorite hobby or a particular sport that they are interested in, you should be able to make appropriate notes of this for future reference. When you happen to speak with them again you can pull up that record and then inquire about that hobby or discuss that particular sport that they are interested in. Simple gestures such as remembering someone's birthday, the names of their children or their favorite restaurant can go a long way to helping you establish a strong rapport with that individual; thus, it is preferable that the software application allows you to capture such information. Another important feature is the ability to merge letters with your contact database. This is an important feature as it allows you to easily create a template letter or document, which can be distributed to certain individuals, that you have identified in your contact database (e.g., by category, by department, etc.). Such letters can be extremely helpful when you have to request specific information from all of your clients, or when you wish to communicate a uniform message to a group of contacts. Last, if your job requires you to be away from the office at all, you should make sure that the application interfaces with your PDA or is portable in some fashion (e.g., installed on your laptop computer). This will allow you to keep track of your appointments, tasks, projects, etc. while you are out on the road or in the field.

As discussed herein, an appropriate software application can act as versatile tool to all young professionals. However, simply having the software application on your PC is not enough. Many people who do have these types of applications, simply fail to make full use of their capabilities, so be sure that you review the user manual for the respective application and understand how each feature works. You want to ensure that you are making full use of the application, so be sure that you study its features well.

Learn To Play Golf

Golf is a game that much of corporate America uses to socialize, network and seal deals. Golf is also a game that is used by many companies to raise funds for various foundations or charities. Learning how the game is played, and developing your skill as a golfer will allow you the opportunity to participate in events and functions where your company's VIP clients, it senior managers and its senior executives will likely be attending. It will open a door of opportunity where you are given what is essentially a captive audience of high-powered individuals. In some cases a young professional may be asked if they would like to participate in such events. In these instances, the young professional needs to know how the game of golf works, some basic game etiquette and other such fundamentals.

Sharing a round of golf with a key client or a high level executive allows you, if not forces you, to get to know each other. Between shots, or while waiting on the tee, personal information concerning families, children, interests, hobbies, etc. are often shared. An exchange of business information concerning your educational background, professional experiences, thoughts and suggestions could also be discussed with relevant playing partners. These few hours of golf could allow you an opportunity to pitch an idea or just simply sell yourself to a high-level executive or prospective client.

Some words of caution here however, do not continuously deluge your playing partner(s) with a laundry list of your new ideas, creative suggestions or a three hour long sales pitch. Rather, plan your strategy ahead of time and select a few key talking points that you would like to cover during your round, and leave it at that. Do not be overly aggressive in terms of selling yourself, your thoughts or your company's products. After all, golf is supposed to be a leisure sport. View the round simply as an opportunity to plant a seed or two in the mind of a high level executive or to make an impression on a VIP client. At the end of the round, hand them your business card and hammer out an acceptable follow-up strategy. Who knows, Monday morning you might be getting a phone call from that executive asking if you have some time to share a cup of coffee in his office talking more about your idea to reduce costs in his division.

Don't Be A Pushover

Don't agree with your manager just because he or she is the boss. If you have a well thought out and intelligent opinion, then stick to it. Disagreeing with your manager may offer you an opportunity to showcase your strength of character, determination and courage. In some cases the issue may escalate into a light confrontation, that is why it is absolutely essential that you support your opinion with facts and concrete evidence. Also, always make it clear that you recognize that they are the boss and will gladly follow their wishes accordingly. Nonetheless, be prepared to discuss the specifics of "why" you feel the way you do. At the end of the day, even if your manager doesn't agree with your perspective he or she will likely have gained more respect for you for standing up to them and intelligently arguing your points.

Given that you are disagreeing with someone of higher authority than you, you have to be courteous and respectful in your approach. Do not raise your voice, get emotional or become critical of the other person's opinion. There are ways that you can disagree with tact and professionalism. Start, by acknowledging the other person's perspective, this will immediately disarm them and help to prevent the issue from becoming too confrontational. Recognize the other person's authority and indicate that you are glad to abide by their wishes, but at the same time respectfully offer your opinion on the matter including the reasons why you feel the way you do. For instance, consider the way in which the following employee approaches a disagreement with their manager:

> *"I see your point of view, and given your experience with this topic, I respect your opinion greatly. Let me also say that I will be happy to proceed in whatever manner you would like me to on this issue. Having said this, I do feel very strongly about this issue, and I'd be somewhat remiss if I didn't share my thoughts with you on the matter…[then proceed to offer your opinion and supporting facts]"*

I cannot stress enough the importance of being able to clearly and concisely articulate your thoughts on why you feel the way that you do. If you are unable to do this, you may come across as if you are just being difficult. If you cannot support your opinion with hard evidence, concrete examples or other supporting information in a diplomatic and professional manner, do not argue your point, because your opinion will be based solely upon pure speculation. Think of your opinion as if it was your kitchen table, and your supporting facts are those four legs that your table is standing on. If you are not capable of providing those supporting facts, you really have nothing to rest on.

I would also suggest that you chose your topics wisely when deciding to disagree with your manager or anyone else of higher authority. You do not want to make it a regular occurrence; otherwise you may be viewed adversely. Be selective when deciding to confront your manager with an opinion different than theirs. Be sure that the issue is material and worthwhile enough to spend the time discussing the topic. It doesn't make any sense to you, or to your manager, to debate her on why you feel that the department holiday party should be held on a Tuesday when she feels it should be on a Wednesday. Be sure the issue is material enough for you to take a stand on it.

Selectively choosing an appropriate opportunity to disagree with your manager can help them to see you as something more than just some recent college graduate or young "know nothing." Being able to debate your manager, or any other senior member of the company, and argue your points in a professional, respectful and intelligent manner will help them see you as someone who is passionate, articulate and courageous enough to speak your mind.

Google Yourself

Thanks to the Internet, we now live in a society that allows anyone with an Internet connection to obtain instantaneous access to an immense amount of information. And thanks to the pinpoint searching accuracy of most Internet search engines, it is exceptionally easy to find information about anyone or anything, at anytime. Moreover, the ability to post information (whether accurately or inaccurately) to the Internet has never been easier. Many handheld devices nowadays contain built in digital cameras that make it very difficult to know when you are being photographed. It may appear that someone is dialing their cell phone, when in fact they are taking a picture of you, perhaps in some less than flattering pose. Whether it is some inappropriate or embarrassing pictures, or whether it is some inflammatory remarks that you had made in a blog, you must be aware that there are literally billions of people with the capacity to view that information, including your prospective employers, co-workers, clients, etc.

You may have forgotten about that time you decided to streak across college campus in a drunken stupor. You may have also been unaware that one of your so-called college buddies secretly took pictures of you and decided to play a prank on you by posting those pictures to a popular web site.

You might have also forgotten about that rabble-rousing college term paper that you wrote, which you posted on the internet, about how capitalism will be the downfall of modern day civilization. If you firmly hold those beliefs I don't imagine that you would be applying for a job at a major financial institution. However, if you are like most college students, your views and beliefs tend to evolve and develop as you grow older, gain more experience, expand your education and study the views and beliefs of others. While your term paper may very well have reflected your beliefs in your sophomore year of college, perhaps that paper is not a true reflection of your current beliefs. After graduation, perhaps you decided to pursue a career in finance, and applied to many major financial institutions, only you forgot about that term paper, which so vehemently criticized our capitalistic society. What if your prospective employer found that paper during the interview process? Clearly, we are all protected by our first amendment rights and I am certainly not saying that you are not entitled to your opinions; however, if you are interested in advancing your career, you need to consider how your employer will interpret your personal opinions, particularly if they run contradictory to the mission of your employer.

Before you start your career searching adventure, make sure that there is no inciting or contradictory information about you on the Internet. Be sure that there is no inappropriate or embarrassing information about you on the Internet. A simple Google search can reveal much of this information. Be sure to Google all possible derivations of your name (e.g., James Smith, Jim Smith, Jimmy Smith, etc.). If you do find information about you on the Internet that is not appropriate or paints you in a poor light, do what you can to have that information removed immediately. If you are unsuccessful or incapable of removing such information, plan a strategy accordingly so that you are prepared to explain the information if you are asked about it by someone.

Do Not Start An Office Pool

Officer pools are fun and entertaining. Whether it is a Super Bowl pool, a NCAA basketball pool or a lottery pool, they are for the most part, harmless and non-disruptive. With some specific limitations that are worth noting, I have generally said that participating in an office pool is acceptable office behavior for a young professional; however, you should not be acting as the official pool organizer. The amount of time and effort utilized to prepare, organize, implement and monitor the pool is much greater that the amount of time and effort that is required to simply participate in one. Therefore, you should not act as the individual who is responsible for developing, organizing or maintaining the office pool. If you are known as the "office pool guy" you run the risk of developing an unfavorable reputation. You may soon become known as someone who does not have enough work to do and someone who spends considerable time in the office on non-office tasks, such as running the office pool.

Another important consideration is to determine who the other participants in the pool are. If middle and upper level managers are typically involved in such pools, this is a rather good indication that the participation in such pools is acceptable conduct in the office. However, if you notice that the great majority of participants in the pool are your peers and co-workers, and there is very little involvement from upper and middle level management, this may be a hidden sign that the participation in such pools is not endorsed by management and is not considered acceptable behavior.

As far as participating in an office pool, for the most part, most traditional sports oriented pools are acceptable pools. A pool trying to guess the sex and weight of a co-workers baby is also acceptable. However, there are some individuals who may wish to make things more interesting or shall we say unique. Some may develop more alternative types of office pools. For instance, there are pools with pre-defined lists of celebrities, world leaders, etc. where the object of the pool is to guess which of the listed individuals will be the next to pass away. Pools of this nature are morbid, inappropriate and should be altogether avoided by every reasonable individual. Use your judgment and a good dose of common sense when deciding whether to participate in an office pool.

Last, be cautious of the amount of time and energy that you will be required to participate in the pool. For instance, simply selecting a box from a grid, handing over a $10 bill to the organizer of the pool and waiting to see the final score of the Super Bowl is one thing. However, try to avoid those types of pools that may require significant time and efforts on your part. For instance, if you are involved in something like an office version of fantasy football, often there will be drafts, trades, statistics monitoring, etc., all of which will require some significant time from you and all of the other participants, which may make it less of an acceptable activity to management.

When dealing with office pools, consider the following tips:

- While it is often acceptable to "participate" in an office pool, never act as the individual who "organizes" the pool. Leave this task to someone else.

- Consider who the participants are. If middle and upper level management routinely participates in such pools, this can be viewed as a sign that the behavior is acceptable. However, if participants typically just include your peers, this can be a sign that management does not endorse the behavior.

- If the pool is in any way distasteful, disrespectful or ill mannered, avoid it entirely.

- Do not engage in office pools that will require a significant amount of your time or efforts.

Learn To Prioritize

Regardless of whether you are a young professional just starting out on your career or an experienced high level executive, the skill of properly prioritizing your work is an essential tool that will help you be successful. Prioritizing your work will help you manage your time and focus your efforts on the tasks that need appropriate attention.

Don't just arrive at the office and start working on some arbitrary tasks. Know what tasks you need to accomplish that day and know how you plan to accomplish them. Plan your work with prudence and discipline. Many of you may be tempted to tackle those insignificant low priority tasks before tackling those more complicated time-consuming tasks, just because they are easier to accomplish and typically require less effort and time. We first tend to address the items that can be easily and swiftly accomplished, not necessarily the items that need the most immediate attention.

As discussed in the "Make Use of Appropriate Software" tip, you can easily prioritize your tasks, assignments and projects with many of the scheduling and planning software applications out on the market today. Many of these applications include priority scales that let you assign priority levels to each task. Many of these applications will also let you create your own priority scale to fit your personal preferences or professional needs.

Without prioritizing your work many young professionals, and seasoned professionals for that matter, can be easily overwhelmed by the number of things that need to be done. Many might have difficulty focusing on the task at hand as they might be thinking about the next task that needs their attention. Many might try working on several tasks all at the same time; however, this strategy rarely works and often results in substandard performance and poor quality of work. Therefore, before you leave the office each night, review your task list and plan the following day accordingly. Decide what tasks need to be completed, what day and/or time they need to be completed by, and how much time you expect to dedicate toward each task. Use your scheduling application to essentially "block off" the appropriate amount of time for those tasks that you intend to focus on for that day. This way you are effectively committing yourself to that particular task for that period of time. In essence, you are agreeing to engage that and only that particular task during that period of time. That way there is no question what you should be doing, and when you should be doing it. This will help prevent you from becoming overwhelmed and will assist you in remaining focused and staying on track throughout the day.

Here are a few tips to help you learn the skill of properly prioritizing your work:

- *Develop a priority scale that suits your needs.* Be sure that there is sufficient granularity in your scale to truly differentiate priority levels.

- *Consider the source.* Consider who issued the directive when assigning a priority level to a task. For instance, a non-technical, non time-sensitive request from a high level senior executive may be as much, if not a higher priority, than a highly technical time-sensitive request from your low-level manager, simply because of who assigned you the task.

- *Set deadlines.* Consider the time sensitiveness of each task and assign an appropriate deadline. Be sure deadlines are reasonable and achievable. If they are not, you may burn yourself out or damage your morale and confidence as performance may often fall short of expectations.

- *Schedule your time and be flexible.* On your calendar, schedule time each day to work on each task or assignment.

- *Know your personal clock.* Schedule high priority tasks during your peak performance times. For instance, if you are a so-called morning person, schedule key tasks and assignments each day during the morning. If you perform better in the afternoon, schedule key tasks and assignments in the afternoon.

- *Differentiate between manager-assigned tasks and self-assigned tasks.* Manager-assigned tasks should always take precedence over any self-assigned projects or tasks. Self-assigned tasks include those tasks, which you have not been specifically asked to do by someone else. Self-assigned tasks are those tasks, which you wish to accomplish yourself through your own self-discipline and initiative.

- *Don't ignore low priority tasks.* Budget some time each day to work on low priority tasks. If you don't you might ignore these tasks to the point where they will ultimately become urgent priorities.

Learn a Foreign Language or Culture

There is no doubting the fact that businesses today, both big and small, are dealing in a truly global economy. There are many reasons why a company may wish to "go global" including more affordable labor or production costs, expanding and developing economies that allow for greater market penetration, greater technical talents with which to select from, etc. Consumers and business are buying and selling goods and services from all over the world. If your company is not buying and selling goods overseas, it may be just a matter of time before it does. Companies today must have the knowledge and wherewithal to compete in this global marketplace. As a young professional you can contribute to your company's success in this global market place by understanding the languages, cultures or customs of the countries that your company develops relations with or does business in.

If a large portion of your company's revenues are generated by one particular foreign nation, it can only assist your chances of moving up the corporate ladder if you are closely familiar with the language and culture of that nation. If your company has a foreign presence, and significant career advancement opportunities were to open up in any such foreign offices, you will be broadening your options and increasing your chances of securing those opportunities if you are familiar with the language and culture of that nation. Even if you do not opt to take that position overseas, there may still be a continuous need for in-house translators and interpreters that can assist other employees in translating conversations, meetings, correspondences, documents, etc. Having your name on a short list of available parties to translate is great exposure and creates good value for you within the organization.

Get Organized

Young professionals can more easily adapt to the frenzied, face-paced and challenging work environment associated with most offices by fully developing their organizational skills. In fact, a young professional's ability to accomplish tasks, meet deadlines, overcome obstacles and ultimately succeed in the corporate world greatly depends upon this essential skill. Developing your organizational skills will not only benefit one professionally, but will also aid the individual by helping to provide order and structure to their personal life as well.

Failure for one to develop appropriate organizational skills can result in substandard workplace performance. In the midst of confusion and disorganization, an individual will often lose their focus or train of thought. Couple this with the added pressure of a tight deadline and individuals particularly unseasoned individuals (e.g., young professionals) will simply fail to achieve their peak performance.

In the tip "Keep A Busy Work Space" we discussed the importance of having your workspace appear "busy." However, as stated in that tip, busy looking does not mean cluttered or messy, and it certainly does not mean disorganized. Many of us are organized in the sense that there is order and structure to how things are stored or filed, but to the eyes of an outsider our workspace may appear disorganized.

Tips for improving your organizational skills include the following:

- *Invest resources in necessary equipment* (e.g., portable email device, PDA, computer databases, CD's (for data storage), notepads, files and folders, etc.).

- *Invest time in developing appropriate filing systems to store necessary information.* Develop a written set of procedures on how your information is filed or stored. This will not only act to solidify your commitment to getting organized, but will also serve to aid your colleagues if any of them need to find anything while you are out of the office.

- *Manage your time wisely.* Knowing what you have to accomplish each day, week or month is only a start. Next you need to know how much time you need to dedicate to each task. You must also be diligent about scheduling fitting times throughout the day to accomplish such tasks.

- *Dedicate a portion of your workspace as an "Active Work Site."* In other words, this particular section of your desk should only be used to store information relating to the task that you are presently engaged in, and nothing else. This will help you stay focused on that specific task and prevent you from being distracted by other assignments or tasks as they are given to you.

Understand Project Management Basics

There is a vast difference between a short-term, often recurring, task such as preparing a monthly report, and a more long-term typically non-recurring task such as enhancing the division's management information systems capacities. Short-term recurring tasks will not typically require much in terms of planning, time or resources. However, the long-term non-recurring tasks may require extensive planning, considerable time and great resources. These longer-term non-recurring tasks are often referred to as "projects." If a young professional is chosen to participate on, or lead, a project team, they will need to understand the intricacies of successful project management. In order to ensure success, projects must be handled in a very methodical manner.

Managing a project requires the project manager to identify the specific objective, coordinate planning, assemble resources, develop strategies, track and monitor progress, motivate team members all within three pre-defined constraints, which include (1) a specific timeframe, (2) monetary budget and of course (3) acceptable quality of the end result. This is sometime referred to as the Project Management Triangle. A good project manager understands these constraints and can overcome them with ingenuity and resourcefulness. A good project manager also understands that each of these constraints is competing against the others and that a change to any one of these constraints will affect the other constraints.

Project managers must also understand the variety of actions that must be employed when administering a project. There are many common tools and practices utilized in successful project management, which can be widely applied in many different types of uses (e.g., manufacturing of automobiles, software development, real estate development, etc.). Given the breadth and depth of the subject matter, I would suggest that young professionals perform some more comprehensive research on their own; however, provided below is a brief list of some key project management tools and practices:

- *Target identification.* Before exerting any efforts and resources elsewhere, be completely sure of what it is that you are expected to accomplish.

- *Assembling of resources.* Determine what resources (e.g., people, skills sets and experiences, technologies, equipment, materials, etc.) you will need to successfully complete the project.

- *Planning and design.* Document the entire workflow of the project and map out key stages in the project.

- *Work breakdown and task assignment.* Assign tasks to project team members, create and communicate expectations of performance including deadlines.

- *Project execution or production.* Ensure team members complete tasks under established guidelines and expectations. Develop and implement applicable motivational and, when necessary, disciplinary methods.

- *Project control and performance monitoring.* Monitor progress and performance through applicable metrics.

- *Problem resolution.* As obstacles are identified, team members should weigh all relevant options, select the most appropriate solution and execute the solution.

- *Project closure.* Prepare final status report. Review project results, discuss whether the project delivered the intended benefit, discuss any relevant lessons learned from the project, etc.

Don't' Be Afraid to Communicate Bad News

As employees, we have a natural inclination to want to please our managers and therefore are much more likely to report things that are good and positive rather than things that are bad or negative. We don't want to be the carrier of bad news, we don't want to second-guess the strategic or technical decisions of senior members and we don't want to seem as though we are making excuses for poor performance. This hesitation to report bad or negative information up the chain of command can often result in a significant disconnect between management and its employees. This breakdown in communication can often lead to inaccurate representations to senior management about how particular operations, applications, processes or people are actually performing.

If you believe that there is a fundamental flaw in a process, software application, procedure, position, etc. you may improve your standing with upper management by bringing this issue to their attention. However, before you do so, be sure that your assessment is validated with research and supporting evidence so as not to misinform or misguide. If your assessment is confirmed by way of additional research and evidence, report the issue to your manager as soon as possible and suggest to him or her that they take your findings into consideration. If your findings ultimately help lead to a resolution, you stand to gain a great deal of political capital by the self-initiated ownership that you will have taken in the issue. Successfully identifying the problem, reporting your findings to the appropriate individuals and ultimately assisting in developing and implementing a solution will help you stand out from the crowd.

Don't Expect Your Manager (or anyone else) To Do "Your" Work

This tip may sound somewhat obvious; however, all too often many young professionals will rely upon someone else to catch and correct their mistakes within their work. Whether you are preparing a report, memorandum, analysis, etc., if you are uncertain about a item or issue, never rely upon someone else to clarify it or correct it without first exhausting all possible resources yourself. Many employees are well aware that their managers or supervisors are going to review and sign off on much of their work; therefore, some young professionals have a tendency to skim over the details, overlook an issue that they are uncertain of, or fail to seek proper resolution to a particular problem. As astounding as this may sound, some individuals simply "give up" and blatantly transfer responsibility for its resolution or clarification to their manager. This is unacceptable and grossly inappropriate if you are expecting to be viewed as a true professional.

When you are confronted with an issue that you are not certain of, or are presented with a problem that you are having some difficulty reconciling, you simply must take all reasonable and rational steps to understand and correct the matter yourself. Such steps may include further review of departmental policies or procedures concerning the issue, performing additional in-depth research and due diligence on the topic at hand or contacting applicable sources (e.g., mentors, co-workers, colleagues, etc.) about the problem.

If after you have exhausted all reasonable efforts you are still unable to better understand the issue or correct the problem, you may seek the advice or guidance of your manager and supervisor; however, you should prompt them of the issue or uncertainly upfront and inform them of the appropriate steps that you have taken to solve the issue yourself. This will advise them that you are not simply "giving up" on the issue, but rather have taken all reasonable courses of action to facilitate its resolution, but have still not been successful and are in need of their assistance.

Follow Up, Then Follow Up Again

As a young professional, you need to learn how to follow up on outstanding issues, uncertainties, questions, etc. that you may encounter while completing a task or working on a project. A young professional who encounters an obstacle while working on a task may be forced to put the task on hold, so that they can get some clarification or direction from a more senior member of the group. If they are unsuccessful in reaching such a senior member of the group initially, they might send an email or leave a voice mail with their question and wait to hear back from them. Many will simply put the task aside until this information is obtained. After all, how can they be expected to continue if they are completely uncertain how to proceed? However, the flaw of many young professionals here is the lack of follow up on the issue until it is fully resolved. The more senior the member of the group in which you are seeking advice or guidance from, the more hectic their schedule will likely be and the more burdened their workload will likely be. Thus, they are more likely to be preoccupied with other more critical tasks, assignments, meetings, etc., which may force them to defer replying to your email or voice mail for some time. Young professionals need to be persistent at following up on such issues. In the initial contact, young professionals should communicate the importance of the task that they are working on and the nature of the deadline that they are working under so that the more senior member is aware of the time sensitivity of the task.

If a young professional fails to meet a deadline or sufficiently complete a task, it is entirely unacceptable and grossly inappropriate to make excuses such as "Well, I had a question and contacted Mr. Smith, but he never returned my call" or "I needed some additional information from the Account Dept., but they never sent it to me." While you may have been forced to place the task on hold until you receive some guidance or assistance of some kind, this does not in any way relieve you of the obligation that you have to complete the task at hand by the assigned deadline. The task was assigned to you, and it is yours to complete; period! If you are unsuccessful at getting the advice, guidance or information you need to complete the task, it is your responsibility, and your responsibility alone, to ensure that you continue to follow up on the outstanding issue, or if necessary, get the advice, guidance or information from somewhere else.

Eat Right

It is no secrete that eating a properly balanced and well-proportioned diet increases your energy level, improves your stamina and enhances your ability to think clearly. Much like the professional athlete that must eat right in order to achieve optimum physical performance on the playing field, young professionals, should continuously strive to eat a properly balanced diet in order to achieve optimum intellectual performance on the playing field of corporate America. This is a simple, yet highly effective, technique that many young professionals who are seeking to advance themselves simply overlook in their daily routines.

Eating a properly balanced diet is essential to improving one's physical and cerebral performance. Equally important is ensuring that meals are eaten at appropriate times throughout the day. In other words, it is best to eat more frequent smaller meals over the course of the day rather than eating fewer larger meals throughout the day. Spacing smaller meals throughout the day not only prevents hunger cravings, which can cause serious disruptions to one's ability to focus and reason but also improves digestive effectiveness and optimizes your body's ability to absorb key nutrients throughout the day.

Your daily diet should also include a multivitamin to ensure that you are getting all of the recommended vitamins and minerals. Additionally, you should ensure that your body remains properly hydrated throughout the day. Proper fluid intake is an essential component to good health and peak performance. Ideally, the average individual should be consuming around eight glasses of water daily.

There is an extraordinary amount of information available on the market today, which discusses this matter in astounding detail. I would strongly suggest that all young professionals speak with their physicians about their dietary habits, and ask for assistance in developing a fitting diet which takes into account the individual's weight, medical history, occupation, etc. In some cases, the services of a certified nutritionist may be of some value to you in this effort. At the very least, all young professionals should perform some additional research on this topic so as to better educate themselves on the importance of this subject. Developing a proper set of dietary habits and implementing them on a consistent basis, day in and day out, will help to improve your performance whether it is in the home, on the basketball court or at the office.

Keep A Spare At The Office

Appearance matters in the corporate world. As a young professional you are not only representing yourself to clients, colleagues, competitors, etc. you are representing your employer and everything that your employer stands for. Many of us might not think twice before hustling yourself into a 2:00 meeting with a key client while wearing a ketchup stained tie compliments of the double cheeseburger that you hastily swallowed ten minutes earlier. However, this is not likely the image that your employer is asking you to represent on their behalf to that potential client.

You might have worked diligently over the last few months preparing for a key presentation before all of senior management. The day of the presentation you might decide to get out of the office, have a nice lunch and just relax a little before the big presentation. Upon your return to the office you might notice a smattering of tomato sauce stains on your crisply pressed white shirt from the poorly chosen dish of spaghetti that you just had for lunch. This is not likely the ideal image that you are trying to convey to those select few individuals who have the power to vastly alter your career.

Much like how many of us carry a spare tire in our car, you should be prepared for the occasional lunch accident, coffee mishap or toner ink debacle all of which can cause havoc to your appearance. Depending upon the extent of the accident and the importance of any meetings, presentations and high profile events that you may have planned for latter in the day, you might find it prudent to change your shirt or put on a new tie. Try keeping a spare shirt, tie, blouse, sweater, etc. in your desk. Similar to the spare tire in your car, you never know when you might need it, but when the time comes you can rest assured that you will be ready.

Lose The Gum

While causally chewing gum may be socially acceptable outside the office, it can be considered adolescent and immature inside the office. When speaking with someone else, chewing gum can impede once speech and distract your listener. Even when you are not speaking with anyone at all, many gum chewers will often crack, pop or snap their gum unbeknownst to themselves, which can greatly annoy other employees, colleagues or clients in the area. While the act of chewing gum may be relatively harmless, one can easily develop an ill-mannered habit of doing it all too often which can be difficult to break. Such a habit could adversely affect other people's opinion of that individual as a professional. Therefore, when at the office, it is best to leave the gum at home.

Contain Your Excitement

When you are rewarded for all of your hard work and extraordinary efforts, whether it is in the form of a promotion, salary increase, large bonus or so forth, do not be overly and outwardly grateful and appreciative. Even though you may be ready to jump out of your chair with excitement and pump your fist in the air, be sure to contain your emotions and enthusiasm while in the presence of your boss and your co-workers. Offer a short and sincere "Thank you for the recognition" and leave it at that. Once you are at home, away from your boss and your co-workers, feel free to pop the champagne and celebrate. If you are overly thankful and appreciative of the recognition, it may appear as though you do not believe that you are fully deserving of such a reward. It may also appear as though this one reward will satisfy your expectation for future rewards, promotions, bonuses, etc. for a long time. With all of your hard work and extra efforts that you have put into your career, you should convey a message that seems to say "Thank you for recognizing my hard work and dedication." You do not want to convey a message that says "Oh my god! I can't believe it, you actually promoted me and you are going to pay me how much?" In other words, don't act like the rookie NFL player who scores a key touchdown and arrogantly taunts and dances himself back to the sidelines. Rather, act like that seasoned NFL veteran player who after a key score simply hands the ball back to the referee and takes their place with the team. In other words, act like you've been there before, and act like your going to be there again.

Containing your enthusiasm has many advantages. It shows your boss that you are a calm, collected and controlled individual. It may also leave your boss guessing that perhaps, you may have been expecting a greater, larger and more lucrative reward, which could leave them thinking about future opportunities for you.

Containing yourself in the presence of your co-workers is also critically important. No one likes a sore winner. Coming out of a meeting with your boss where you just received a promotion that everyone in the office was hoping for can cause some tension amongst the group. Standing on your chair and screaming at the top of your lungs in celebration is poor corporate sportsmanship and will only serve to distance yourself from your co-workers. Maintaining a strong and productive rapport with your co-workers is critical as it will help to prevent adverse chatter and gossip about your character, your capabilities, your work ethic, etc., some of which could ultimately find it's way to, and adversely influence, other key decision makers within the organization who possess the authority and wherewithal to affect your career.

Additionally, as you are promoted, you may very well need the support and efforts of your co-workers in order to carry out your new responsibilities. Show a level of graciousness and respect as you receive your special recognition and you will be doing yourself a great service in helping to preserve a strong and fruitful relationship with those that still may have the power to support (or destroy) your reputation within the group or the organization.

Consider Departmental Value

As you are reviewing your career plans, designing an appropriate strategy to advance within the organization and considering other employment opportunities within the organization, young professionals must consider many things. In many cases, employees will switch jobs within a company because they are unchallenged and are looking for more interesting work, they want higher compensation or they don't like their boss. However, all too often young professionals fail to consider these opportunities from a broader organizational, perspective. Failure to do so can often have serious consequences on an employee's future growth potential.

When considering other opportunities, young professionals should consider how valuable the department, division or group is to the entire organization. Departments, divisions or groups that fail to contribute to the company's overall profitability or those that are not a key component of the Company's core mission are typically working under much more restricted budgets and therefore, less likely to experience rapid growth and expansion. Without rapid growth and expansion, future employment opportunities within that department, division or group are typically slower to develop, and may even be subject to contraction. Departments that are strong contributors to the organization's earnings are more likely to gain the benefit of larger budgets and financial resources, which help to facilitate greater employment opportunities in the future. Thus, employees in these fast growing departments will generally have a greater selection of future employment opportunities, which are typically better suited to their individual backgrounds, than most other areas of the organization.

When interviewing for opportunities in other areas of the organization, young professionals should inquire about these matters. Young professionals should ask the interviewer how the return on assets (ROA) of the group compares to the ROA of other areas of the organization. Young professionals should ask how committed the parent entity and its senior management is to the respective department. Consider how long the department has been in existence. Young professionals should directly inquire about existing and anticipated growth opportunities within the department. Young professionals should ask about the true mission or purpose of the department, and consider how this relates to the overall corporate mission or purpose. When considering a move to another area of the organization, young professionals must be sure to do all of their homework in order to fully assess the opportunity.

Be Cautious About Breaking the Chain of Command

Much like the military, corporate America has an established chain of command, and young professionals should understand it, respect it and abide by it. Every employee, even the President and CEO has a superior to whom they report. Circumventing your immediate superior and seeking approval, guidance or support from other more superior members of the organization is not advised and should be avoided whenever reasonably possible.

Those who circumvent the authority of their immediate supervisor can certainly be perceived poorly by their direct supervisor, but also by their co-workers and other senior members of the company. If you have an issue with your immediate supervisor, are failing to receive proper recognition, feel as though you are not being rewarded properly or feel as though you are being grossly mistreated, the first thing you should do is take a deep breath, then objectively and unemotionally determine whether the issue is truly a materially significant issue. If you convince yourself that the issue is significant enough to pursue, you should then start to compile a comprehensive written list of your complaints or criticisms. Be sure that you are capable of supporting your claims with concrete examples and specific facts. Once you have done this, ask if you can speak with your immediate supervisor or manager about the issue. In the meeting, be specific about your concerns or complaints. Do not be generic and vague. Do not simply state, I don't feel as though I am being properly recognized. Be specific and give specific examples of events or instances that support your claim. Also, couch your concerns or complaints in the context of wanting to improve or develop as a professional. For instance, you might say to your supervisor "I noticed last week that you sent out a congratulatory email to the staff about Joe's hard work on the ABC Co. account, and that you didn't mention my involvement. I just wanted to let you know that I was equally involved in obtaining that account, and if you feel that I didn't deserve the same recognition, it would help me focus my energies and efforts on improving my abilities if I knew why you felt that way." Present the issue in the context of wishing to improve yourself as a professional, rather than simply presenting a complaint to your manager.

Taking a proactive approach with your immediate supervisor or manager will benefit you in many ways. First, this will show them (1) that you are interested and passionate enough about improving your abilities (as you are seeking guidance on improving), (2) that you are acutely aware how your manager, and others, perceive you and your abilities (thus, the need to address the outstanding issue), and (3) that you are assertive enough to speak up when you feel as though you have not been treated properly. Most supervisors will be more than receptive in discussing the situation with you and offering their thoughts and guidance. They are therefore more likely to be in tune with your needs and desires in the future.

If your supervisor is confrontational or unreceptive to your feelings, my suggestion is to let it go for the time being, but to keep a detailed record of the event and the actions that you took to address the situation. If similar situations develop with your supervisor, approach them once again to discuss the issue with them, and record the event and the outcome in your records. If your supervisor still cannot persuade you that the way they acted was appropriate or if they are still unreceptive to your concerns then, and only then, should you start thinking of alternative strategies. However, before you go over your manager's head, check in with one or two of your loyal colleagues who are familiar with the situation and inquire from them whether they feel your complaints are founded or not. Ask them to be honest and objective about the situation. Make it clear that you do not want "morale support" but rather a candid assessment of the situation. This will help to validate your concerns from an objective and independent perspective. Only after you have noticed a consistently adverse pattern of behavior or conduct from your supervisor, and have confirmed your complaints or criticisms from some of your trusted and independent parties, should you seriously consider circumventing your immediate supervisor's authority.

Nonetheless, I cannot stress enough the importance of not overreacting. Do not go over your boss's head, because of one or even two minor events happened to make you mad or upset. If you do decide to go over your boss's head, be sure that it is a worthwhile issue and not simply a matter of ego or principle. Also you had better be darn sure that your claims are legitimate. Managers do make mistakes, they do make errors and they can overlook the efforts of some of their employees. Give them the benefit of doubt initially. If you do decide to seek the guidance or advice of a more senior member of the organization, it is absolutely critical that you have a comprehensive and detailed written record illustrating all of the specific claims and allegations, as well as a list of all of the actions that you have taken up to this point to address the situation with your immediate supervisor or manager first. This will show the senior member of the organization that these issues are serious enough for you to monitor them and will also validate your concerns or complaints. As you did with your supervisor, if you do decide to speak with a senior member of the organization, adopt the same strategy as you did with your supervisor and stress your desire for more specific feedback or direction so that you can focus your efforts on improving as a professional. Present the issue as a legitimate desire to improve your professional capacities. Do not present the issue as a complaint or grievance.

Suggested tips when deciding to circumvent the chain of command are as follows:

- Take a deep breath, step back from your emotions, and determine how truly significant the issue is. Try to discount issues of pure ego or principle and focus on those issues, which are material to your reputation, performance record, etc.

- If the issue is significant enough, start preparing your thoughts on the matter including what it is exactly that you are upset about. Be sure that you can support your complaints with concrete examples and hard facts.

- Ask to meet with your manager about the issue. Be specific about why you feel the way you do. Present your complaints or criticisms in a way that is positive. Such as, "I really would like to know why you didn't select me to make the presentation to Senior Management. If there are areas you think I need to improve upon, I would really like to know what they are so that I can focus on improving them."

- If you are not satisfied with the meeting, let it pass for the time being, but continue keeping a written record of similar situations that occur including the dates they occurred and the actions (e.g., meeting with supervisor) that you took to address the situation. As other similar situations occur, ask to meet with your supervisor again, to reiterate your concerns in a similar manner.

- If after some time, you are still not satisfied with the response, or lack thereof, from your immediate manager or supervisor, and you are convinced that the issue is significant enough to circumvent their authority, seek the guidance and opinion of a trusted colleague or two who are familiar with the situation. Be sure they give you their honest and objective opinion on the issue.

- Before speaking with a senior member of the organization, you must be sure that you have a written record of all of the events that have occurred and all of the specific actions that you have taken up to this point to address the matter. When speaking with the senior member of the organization, rather than pointing fingers at your immediate manager, present your concerns in a similarly positive manner as you did with your supervisor (e.g., wishing to improve your skills or abilities and would like more specific feedback or guidance). This will help the senior member of the organization see you as an employee concerned about their individual growth and development rather than a tattletale or crybaby.

Never Strong-Arm Your Employer

Never attempt to strong-arm your employer into a raise or a promotion. Some employees may opt to search for other more lucrative employment opportunities out in the market place, and once they have secured an offer they use this as leverage to negotiate a raise or a promotion with their existing employer. If the quality of your work is good, if your work ethic is strong and if you are held in high regard by management, your employer may be willing to match your offer from the competing organization; however, young professionals who decide to pursue this strategy are advised that this strategy can place a dark cloud over your head for a very long time. Pursuing other employment opportunities out in the market while serving your existing employer can classify you as a non-loyalist and someone who has not truly bought into your company's core mission, values and beliefs. No one likes to be pushed up against a wall and threatened, and that is exactly what an employee would be doing to his or her employer in such a situation. If you are searching for other employment opportunities, do not give the slightest indication to your manager or any of your co-workers that you are even considering other outside opportunities. If you have decided to leave, commit to it, be gracious and diplomatic about the opportunity that your manager and employer has given you, and do not look back. Counter offers should rarely be accepted.

A great shortcoming of many young professionals today is that they place so much emphasis on the size of their paycheck and not enough emphasis on the value of other forms of benefits. If you become aware that there are other more lucrative opportunities in the marketplace for work that is similar to yours, be sure to consider all of the other benefits offered, not just the salary. For instance, how do other benefits compare to your current employer's (e.g., quality of health benefits, 401k program, bonus program, employee stock option program, profit sharing, vacation time, etc.)?

You also need to consider whether this new opportunity is suitable to your future career needs. For instance, how does the prospective employer compare to my current employer with regards to opportunity for advancement within the group, division, organization, etc? Is the quality of the personnel adequate to provide me with sufficient opportunities to be thoroughly mentored and developed in my particular discipline? How much of a focus does each of these companies place on employee training and development? How committed is the parent entity or holding company to sustaining the existence of the particular group or division that I would be working in? In other words, is there a possibility that this division or group might be sold, downsized or completely dissolved in the near future? Aside from the salary, young professionals must be sure to take all of these items into full consideration if they are considering a job change.

If you decide to leave your employer, you must be sure that you do so only after you have gained the applicable knowledge and done your appropriate due diligence. If you are offered another opportunity at a different employer and are truly committed to pursuing that opportunity, do so. Never use this as leverage to strong-arm or threaten your current employer into making a counter offer or any other type of inducement to stay.

Be Patient, and Watch the Job Hopping

There is much evidence indicating that generation Y'ers and future generations are likely to switch jobs many times throughout their career. I have read in many cases that the average generation Y'er will switch jobs about 12 times throughout their career. This is in stark contrast to the baby boomers, and earlier generations, that typically have held many less jobs throughout the careers. The absence of corporate loyalty in today's young workforce is likely due to many factors. In part, it may be attributed to the lack of loyalty shown by many companies to its employees by way of the many well-publicized layoffs, downsizings or reductions in retirement or health benefits. Some of this so called corporate disloyalty may also be due to the greatly expanding disparity in pay between the many "average" workers (including entry level, lower and even middle level managers) and high-level executives. Notwithstanding the large salaries that are often earned by most executives, many companies continue to reward corporate executives with generous bonuses, lucrative stock options, and other perks and benefits even when the respective company performs poorly. Still, some of this lack of loyalty may also be attributed to the increasing materialistic society in which we live in. Houses have gotten bigger and more extravagant, the cars we drive have gotten bigger, faster and sportier, designer clothes and accessories are more trendy and more expensive than ever before, technological toys and gadgets are more ubiquitous than ever before, exotic vacations to far away locations are more frequent, etc. Many young professionals seem to gauge the level of their success by the extent of their materialistic possessions. In an effort to be perceived as successful by their family, friends and peers, the spending habits of today's young workforce often greatly exceed their means.

As such, many young professionals are constantly seeking other opportunities at other employers just to earn an extra 10%, 15% or 20% in compensation, without fully considering the long-term consequences of these decisions. However, in the end, a 10%, 15% and even a 20% increase in their salary is not likely to have a significant effect on their financial position. Nonetheless, many young professionals fail to appreciate the opportunities that may exist at their current employers, opportunities that have been built upon their hard work and diligence, opportunities that may soon be capitalized on by way future promotions or salary increases.

Many young professionals simply fail to understand how their "credibility meter" works. As one dedicates their time and effort toward a position, a department and an employer, they begin to develop a reputation for themselves. They begin to develop political capital by way of their accomplishments. They begin to develop their credibility within the organization. The more they achieve, the greater their credibility within that organization. Their credibility cannot be quantified, but it does have value. More importantly, the employee's credibility cannot be transferred to another employer. In other words, once an employee decides to take a new position at a different employer, their credibility meter is automatically reduced to zero, and the process of building that credibility must begin again. In essence, while an employee who decides to pursue another employment opportunity at a different company may be earning an extra few dollars in their paycheck, they are quite literally back to square one in terms of developing a favorable reputation for themselves. When making such a drastic career decision, many young professionals often fail to recognize and fully consider the intangible value associated with their credibility at their current employer. In fact, in many cases, employees may accept a position at a new employer and resign their current positions only to find out that they were in the process of being promoted anyway at their current employer.

Many young professionals are simply not patient enough to give their career advancing strategies sufficient time to work effectively. Many young professionals will chase a slightly bigger paycheck at another company, but not take into consideration the value of the credibility and political capital that they have developed at their current employer. This credibility and political capital will ultimately be converted to additional monetary compensation at some point in the near future if the employee is patient enough and gives their career advancing strategies a reasonable period of time to take effect. However, when switching to a new employer, that young professional must start anew at building a favorable reputation for himself or herself. This effort is not easily accomplished and can be long and arduous as accomplishments must be achieved, competence must be proven, intelligence must be adequately demonstrated, etc.

I recognize that if a young professional has spent many years in the same position with the same company and has no identifiable room to advance, or if an employee has failed to developed material credibility for themselves or has been unsuccessful at creating any political capital for themselves, that switching employers may be a viable and prudent option. However, here I am talking about those employees who know that they are making progress in developing their reputations and creating value for themselves within the organization, but will still routinely skip from one employer to another. Many young professionals fail to give their employer more than a year or two before they start pursuing other opportunities. This can be dangerous as it fails to show a certain degree of stability. For instance, if they have left each of their last three jobs within two years of their hire, how long can we reasonably expect them to stay with us? Does it make sense to invest our time and resources in someone who is not likely to spend more than a year or two with our organization?"

At some point in their careers, young professionals must be aware of the consequences of this so-called job-hopping. Young professionals have to be patient enough to give their career advancing strategies a chance to work.

Never Stop Learning

Young professionals need to take great initiative in terms of fostering their own personal and professional development. Do not expect that someone else will teach you everything that you are going to need to know in your position or throughout your career. Budget restrictions in many large companies have resulted in the elimination or substantial reduction of most management trainee programs. These restrictions and the incessant demand for increased productivity in today's fiercely competitive marketplace simply do not afford many companies the luxury of spending millions of dollars each year to have new employees sit in a corporate classroom for their first six months of employment. In many companies, employees are often hired, given a brief orientation, thrown into their position and placed under the same performance expectations as those who have many more years of experience. Terms such as "sink or swim" and "learn or burn" refer to the manner in which many young professionals are forced to adapt to their new responsibilities.

The absence of formal training and development mechanisms and the importance of getting up to speed quickly largely forces young professionals to take it upon themselves to learn what they need to know in order to do their job well, enhance their knowledge base and grow their skill set. All too often, young professionals can find themselves caught up in the short-term day-to-day demands of completing routine assignments and fulfilling their daily responsibilities, that they lose sight of the larger longer-term perspective, which is to ultimately develop their skills, enhance their knowledge base and increase their value to the organization.

Young professionals should dedicate a certain amount of time each day, week, month and year towards gaining certain knowledge and strengthening their skills. This necessitates a strong work ethic and a disciplined and dedicated focus, as the majority of these studies will likely need to be performed on the employee's personal time. However, before you start searching out materials to study, the first thing you should do is develop a structured and focused curriculum or study plan. What is it exactly that you wish to learn more about? How will this knowledge base help you? Where can I find the resources to give me this knowledge? When do I want to complete these studies? Establishing appropriate deadlines to complete the studies is essential because it creates an expectation of performance, even if only it is a self-imposed deadline. If you fail to meet your prescribed deadlines, increase your focus and dedication to your studies, and pledge to yourself that you will make some certain personal sacrifice if you miss the next deadline.

Once you have developed an appropriate curriculum, you should ask to meet with your manager and share this plan with them. Indicate that you intend on fulfilling these studies on your own time, but that you would appreciate their guidance or direction on the plan. This will place your strong work ethic on display for your manager to see and will serve as notice that you may not necessarily be content on serving in your current position for too long, but rather that you have aspirations of advancing.

Ask your manager for their input on your study plan, particularly whether they feel that these topics will benefit you in advancing your career within the group, division and organization. Adjust the plan as necessary, based upon the conversations you have with your manager. Ask them if they could recommend any good reference materials such as text books, training materials, self-study training programs, trade publications, web sites, seminars, etc.

Listed below is a very brief example of how a curriculum or study plan might look. This one includes only two topics that this employee identified for development; however, depending upon what knowledge you wish to gain and what skills you wish to develop, your study plan may consist of many more topics.

Self Study Plan – John Smith, Junior Accountant			
Topic	**Purpose**	**Source**	**Deadline**
Corporate Financial Statement Analysis	To improve my effectiveness in my current position by allowing me to better identify potential cross selling opportunities in corporate banking.	Financial Analysis, Self Study training program. Relevant text books, Relevant articles, Etc.	End of year 2008
Public Speaking	To become more confident and persuasive in presenting ideas to management. To become more effective at speaking during quarterly department meetings.	Public Speaking Class. Self-Practice Exercises.	End of year 2008

In addition to developing your personal study plan, be guided by the following principles:

- Keep this study plan with you in your brief case, and review it regularly to keep your focus.

- Keep a written record of each action you take toward meeting these objectives. If you read a particular book on a topic in your plan, write it down. If you take a seminar or listen to an audio conference on one of your topics, write it down.

- At the end of the year, or during your performance evaluation with your manager, you can sit down with them and share all of the steps that you have taken (on your own time, and under you own direction) to better yourself as a professional. By writing down all of the steps that you have taken towards completing your personal study plan, you will also be able to reflect on how much, or how little, you have actually accomplished in terms of growing your skills and knowledge.

After you have successfully completed your study plan, develop a new study plan concerning larger, more sophisticated and more material topics that concern your position or profession. Continue this learning cycle throughout your entire career. Never stop seeking greater knowledge.

The corporate world is highly dynamic. New industries are constantly emerging, old industries are constantly changing, regulatory and legal frameworks are always transforming, technologies are constantly improving, management techniques and competitive strategies are always evolving. There shall never be a day that you will know everything there is to know about your profession, so never stop learning. Here are a few key points to summarize this tip:

- Take the initiative in developing your talents, expanding your knowledge base and growing your skill set. Do not rely upon your employers, or anyone else, to deliver this knowledge to you.

- Develop a self-study plan that is tailored toward your current position, as well as your future career aspirations.

- Establish specific deadlines on when you wish to complete these studies, and stick to them. Discipline yourself when a deadline is missed and reward yourself when one is met.

- Share your self-study plan with your manager and seek their feedback.

- Review your study plan often to stay focused on your long-term growth and development objectives, rather than simply handling your day-to-day responsibilities.

- Create daily, weekly, monthly and annual action plans that relate to these studies, and keep a written record of all steps taken toward achieving your self-study objectives.

- Regularly discuss with your manger what steps you have taken to meet your self-study objectives and improve yourself as a professional.

Seek Higher Education

Advanced degrees are all too common nowadays. This can make it difficult for anyone without an advanced degree to move up the organizational ladder. The good news is that many large companies often have tuition reimbursement programs, which will reimburse employees seeking such degrees, whether in part or in whole. This makes it an easier decision for the employee since out of pocket costs can be greatly reduced. Granted, there is a rather substantial commitment that must be required from the employee in terms of time and effort to obtain an advanced degree; however, the future benefits will greatly outweigh the short-term sacrifices.

Clearly there are significant differences between the value of an advanced degree from a top tier institution versus a lower tier institution; however, simply having any type of an advanced degree, regardless of what type of an institution it came from, is a considerable advantage over those employees who do not have a advanced degree at all.

If your employer does not have a tuition reimbursement plan, and you are seriously interested in pursuing a long-term career with your employer, I would suggest that you discuss your interest in obtaining an advanced degree with your manager and ask if the institution could make an exception in your case. The worst that can happen is that they say "no." At the very least, even if your employer cannot accommodate you with your request, you will be making a deliberate announcement to your manager and to other members of the management team, that you value higher education and are seriously interested in developing your knowledge base so as to benefit not only yourself, but the company as well.

If your employer simply cannot accommodate you with any type of a tuition reimbursement program, and you can somehow find a way to afford the advanced degree yourself, pursue it on your own. In an effort to make the process somewhat more financially feasible, try soliciting assistance from your parents or other family members for a loan. Other methods that you could try to make it easier to obtain an advanced degree on your own might include finding and securing appropriate scholarships, taking out student loans, attending a lower cost institution or spreading the courses out over a longer period of time.

In any event, having an advanced degree, or simply working toward one, regardless of where you will obtain the degree from and regardless of how long it might take you is more or less a necessity in today's corporate environment if you are seriously interested in advancing your career.

Keep Your Resume' Updated

Your resume is an abbreviated version of your educational and professional accomplishments, as well as a list of your technical skills and abilities. Having an updated resume' is important since it is a required document as you pursue additional career opportunities, whether they be internal or external. Many people fail to keep their resume' current. Rather they will often update their resume' only after they have decided to pursue another employment opportunity. Haphazardly attempting to assemble a current and relevant version of your resume on a moments notice can often fail to reflect your true experiences, accomplishments and abilities. You may easily overlook a significant accomplishment that you achieved some time ago, or you may have neglected to recall that significant certification that you received last year. While you may be well aware of your day-to-day duties and responsibilities in your current position, you may have some difficulty in presenting them, with clarity, in an abbreviated fashion, particularly when pressed for time. This is precisely why you should have a copy of your resume' available and commit yourself to updating it routinely. I would suggest that you review your resume every few months and ask yourself whether you have achieved any significant accomplishments over this time which deserve to be noted on your resume'. Cross-reference your resume with a running list of your professional accomplishments to ensure that you do not overlook any of your significant achievements.

As many have said, a young professional's resume' should rarely exceed one page in length, to which I generally agree. Therefore, as you routinely update your resume, you will notice how your resume' will continuously evolve. The evolution of your resume' is a reflection of your own individual evolution as a professional. In the early part of your career, the centerpiece of your resume' may have been your extraordinary grade point average from college. However, as time passes and as you gain more experience and knowledge as a professional, this will no longer suffice. Your resume must develop just as you will develop as a professional.

Never Burn Bridges

As you pursue new opportunities, whether in the same company or at other companies, young professionals should never burn a proverbial bridge with their managers, co-workers or colleagues. While you may have despised working for a former manager, you never really know if your professional paths may cross again sometime; therefore, when speaking with others be cautious about the source of your frustrations. You should play your decision to move to another division or department as a better opportunity to develop your skills and advance your career. You should not leave your current department or your current employer in a blaze of glory taking down everyone who ever rubbed you the wrong way. Be diplomatic and professional as your depart and you stand a greater chance of salvaging a relationship that may have some future value. You never know if you might wish to return to the company or department that you are leaving so be careful about what you say before leaving.

Young professionals are not typically accustomed to the rigors of a faced paced, high intensity, extremely competitive work environment associated with much of corporate America. Thus, they are less experienced in handling stressful relationships and criticism. As a result, they are more inclined to talk bad about their manager or supervisor during an exit interview. However, many employees come and go, many markets and industries are small and close-knit, many companies merge and you just never really know who may know whom. Therefore, it may not be that unusual for you to run into your former manager at different company one day, and it is certainly not that unusual if you were to bump into him or her at a trade related event or function. Even though you may detest them, young professionals need to be trained to control their emotions when speaking about former managers, supervisors or other colleagues. Typically a former manager or supervisor will have greater contacts throughout the industry, simply because or their length of experience and involvement in the industry. As such, you do not want to risk them "blacklisting" you with their industry contacts. Doing so may make it difficult for you to develop meaningful professional relationships. Also, you may be interviewing for a job at a different company, where your prospective manager knows your former manager. If so, your prospective manager will likely consult with your former manager about you and your background. You don't want your prospective manager to find out that you went down in venomous, hate filled and immature exit interview at your last position, so be sure to part gracefully and quietly.

Have Fun

As strange as this might seem to some, the final tip I can offer to those starting out on this amazing journey of knowledge and experience, the last bit of advice I can submit to those of you commencing your voyage of professional growth and development is simply to have fun with your labors. Don't view your job and its responsibilities as a dreadfully necessary burden you must endure for the next several decades, because that is not what your job represents. In fact, your work is quite the opposite. View your job as a tool that can be used to create the skills, talents and abilities necessary for you to succeed not only in the corporate world but also in life. View your job and its responsibilities as a sacred instrument, which can be used to shape and mold yourself into that certain someone that you always wanted to become.

Try diligently to view your job, its responsibilities and its challenges as a privileged and honored use of your time. By viewing the context of your work in a constructive and fruitful manner, you are more likely to take much greater pleasure in your day-to-day responsibilities. You may find this difficult, particularly if your day is consumed with monotonous and unchallenging tasks that drain your passion and dilute your enthusiasm. However, regardless of what your responsibilities are, try to recognize each day you step into the office as a limitless opportunity. Each day you step into the office is a day that you stand to refine an existing skill, learn a new skill, meet someone new and exciting, gain new experiences, participate on a team, solve a problem, and become a greater professional. Each day you step in the office is a day to challenge yourself. Challenge yourself to go above and beyond what others expect of you. Challenge yourself to go above and beyond what you expect of yourself. Challenge yourself to try something you never thought you were capable of. Challenge yourself to face your fears. Challenge yourself to do the "impossible." Challenge yourself to become something that you never thought you could become. The corporate world is your blank canvass and your job is your paintbrush. Your ability to create a masterpiece hinges on nothing more heavier than your perseverance, dedication, commitment and positive frame of mind toward your work.

The point I am trying to make is best described in the famous phrase by the French philosopher Rene' Discartes who said *"cogito ergo sum."* In translation this means, "I think, therefore I am." Many people simply fail to truly appreciate the opportunities that their work provides for them in terms of personal and professional growth and development. Having the opportunity to hold meaningful conversations with your colleagues, having the opportunity to solve difficult problems, having the opportunity to contribute your intellect and opinion to a group are opportunities that should be cherished and appreciated, not protested and criticized. Much like how physical fitness exercises our muscles and makes them stronger, your career and your journey through corporate America will exercise your mind and strengthen your character, so you should not protest your job, rather you should celebrate it and the opportunities it presents to you. If you are capable of this one simple thing, and nothing else, I promise you a future filled with joy, satisfaction and true success.

I wish you well on your journey.

Have fun!

www.ingramcontent.com/pod-product-compliance
Lightning Source LLC
Chambersburg PA
CBHW020202200326
41521CB00005BA/225